Allowances DOLLARS and SENSE

A PROVEN SYSTEM FOR TEACHING YOUR KIDS About Money

PAUL W. LERMITTE

McGraw-Hill
Ryerson

Toronto Montréal New York Burr Ridge Bangkok Bogotá Caracas
Lisbon London Madrid Mexico City Milan New Delhi Seoul
Singapore Sydney Taipei

McGraw-Hill
Ryerson Limited

A Subsidiary of The **McGraw·Hill** Companies

ISBN: 0-07-560929-0

34567890 MP 050403020100
Printed and bound in Canada.

Canadian Cataloguing in Publication Data

Lermitte, Paul W.
  Allowances dollars and sense: a proven system for teaching your kids about money

Includes index.
ISBN 0-07-560929-0

1. Children – Finance, Personal – Study and teaching. I. Title.

HG179.I47   1999   332.024'054   C99-930670-7

Publisher: **Joan Homewood**
Editorial Co-ordinator: **Catherine Leek**
Production Co-ordinator: **Susanne Penny**
Editor: **Tita Zierer**
Cartoons: **Justin David Nichols**
Electronic Page Composition: **FiWired.com**
Cover Design: **Sharon Matthews**
Back Cover Photograph: **Jeff Weddell**

Dedicated to
Ryan, Patrick and Jeremy
who we are blessed to care for,
guide, and love.

ACKNOWLEDGMENTS

In pulling this project together, I have two people I am truly thankful to:

First, I wish to gratefully acknowledge the assistance of Bill Bishop, president of Bishop Information Group Inc., in the writing of this book. (He is the author of two books on digital marketing.) His advice, direction and writing expertise helped make this a great book.

Secondly, I want to thank my wife Jan, whose literary genius has always awed me. She amazed me as we worked through the tight and difficult times. Her love and encouragement pushed me to the completion of my manuscript.

There are many others that I wish to thank: family, friends and colleagues who have offered me support over the course of my career.

Thank you to Dan Williams and Paul Stevens who first encouraged me to put into words 'my financial adventure with my kids'!

Thank you to Dan Sullivan for being my business coach for ten years along with his partner Babs Smith. Their example inspired me to write this book and their program gave me the support to make it happen. Their Strategic Coach Program — a lifetime focusing program for highly successful entrepreneurs — has been a significant influence in my life. I would also like to thank Ross, Dorie, Shannon, Paulette, Susan and the entire Strategic Coach team.

Thank you to Adrienne Waller and Peter Stewart, my good friends, who have done a lot of listening and have been my objective mentors in so many aspects of life.

Thank you to Dr. John Patterson for his input in the early stages of my writing. He is author of the book, *Russian Roulette-Gambling with Disability*.

Thank you to the Nichols: to Justin for his great drawings and to Mike and Nancy for consistently refreshing my spirit.

Thank you to my terrific business partner, Sherry L. Cavallin, whose wisdom, friendship, and support over the past sixteen years have been invaluable. Also to her husband and my good friend, Fred Cleutinx.

Thank you to my business associates, Kim, Connie, Dave, Rebecca, Traci, Elise, Sara, Anil, Margo, Sunny, Kelly, Susan, Cathie and Mike. Without their help and encouragement I could not have continued to live this great adventure.

Thank you to a number of wonderful people who have given me inspirational ideas throughout my fifteen years of financial planning: Dave and Shirley, Jim and Darlene, Hermann and Vivien , Mike and Pat, Alan and Margaret, Wayne and Mary, and Andrea.

Thank you to all the McGraw-Hill Ryerson gang: Joan, Suzanne, Cathy, Tita, Claudia, Teresa and Jodi, who helped make my dream a reality.

And very importantly, I want to thank my father and mother, Dick and Norma, who inspired me from an early age to be an entrepreneur, by encouraging me as I sold newspapers, mowed lawns, baby-sat and tried other small ventures. Their love and support has been and continues to be a stable foundation in my life.

Also, I wish to thank my three sisters, Carol, Dianne and Christine, for choosing to be close friends as we grew up, and for being competitive and adventurous in spirit in a way that seemed to motivate each of us to excel.

Thank you to our three sons, Ryan, Patrick and Jeremy, who have blessed our lives enormously. They have stretched us in ways we simply could not have imagined. Although the future is full of risks, I am confident that our lives together will include many more adventures and milestones.

Finally, I wish to thank my Lord Jesus Christ, who gives me hope, forgiveness and love, today and each day ahead.

> *"Train a child in the way he should go*
> *and when he is old he will not turn from it."*
> — Proverbs 22:6

TABLE OF CONTENTS

Kids and Money:

Building A Solid Foundation

As a professional financial planner, I thought I would have no trouble coaching my kids to handle money responsibly. But seven years ago, when I decided to give my three sons an allowance to buy candy, toys, running shoes, rollerblades and a million other things, I was just like every other parent. I didn't know where to start or what steps to take. My lack of expertise really surprised me. So my wife and I set out to learn how to teach our kids to handle money. We have used a variety of techniques, and our boys have developed confident money-management skills. In the past seven years, I have developed and refined a complete program to teach my kids about money. I call this The Making Allowances System. My wife and I have been extremely pleased with the results, and this system has also worked for scores of our friends, relatives and associates.

Over the years, I have observed that many adults don't know how to handle money responsibly. I believe this is because they didn't handle money enough when they were children. Their parents did all of the spending, banking and saving. They may have received an allowance, but it was used to make small purchases, and unfortunately, they may never have learned how to save money for more expensive items, or for long-term investments. No wonder many adults in our society are hooked on credit cards and live month by month spending all of their income. They never learned some basic money skills as children.

If you want your children to grow up to be financially responsible adults, I believe you must let them handle money often. At an early age, they need to handle money and understand the importance of depositing money in a bank on a regular basis. They also need to develop the habit of saving money for major purchases. These lessons will help your children develop a much more comprehensive understanding of money and how to manage it. In fact, I believe that giving an allowance sets the groundwork for good money management because it provides an opportunity for parents to help their children develop good habits that will stay with them for life. If you can teach your children to save, spend and invest responsibly, you will prepare them for a productive, successful life.

In this book, I share with you what I've learned about teaching kids about money. But before I get into the details of The Making Allowances System, I'd like to help you identify the dangers and opportunities you face as a parent in regard to your kids and money.

Kids and Money: The Dangers

As a parent, you face six key dangers if you don't have a system for teaching your kids healthy habits and attitudes about money.

DANGER 1
Financial Dependency

Your children could become financially irresponsible adults. If you don't teach your children properly about money, they could grow up with poor money skills. They may end up spending every cent they earn, living pay cheque to pay cheque. They could become mired in debt or, even worse, they could remain financially dependent on you when you should be saving for, or enjoying your retirement. In fact, how you teach your kids about money now could affect your own personal wealth in the future.

DANGER 2
Destructive Values

Your children could adopt destructive values about money. In today's complex, consumer-oriented, media-saturated world, your kids may adopt values about money which completely contradict the values you hold. For example, they may come to equate money with self worth. They may become hooked on possessions, on keeping up with the crowd, on always staying in fashion. They may adopt the attitude that you are always available to bail them out when they need money; that if they want something, all they need to do is ask for it. They may develop unrealistic expectations, believing that they are entitled to all the latest trends and their happiness depends on having them.

DANGER 3
The Debt Trap

Your children may grow up to have bad money habits and possibly end up in paralizing debt. If you don't teach your kids about money when they're young, they could grow up to be victims of our credit and consumer culture. It's possible they could enter their 20s and 30s not knowing how to set financial goals, how to save money for the future, how to make a budget, how to plan buying decisions and how to be a smart consumer. Newspapers often carry stories of young adults on the financial brink of disaster.

DANGER 4
Loss of Confidence

Without positive money habits and good life skills, your children could become adults lacking the confidence to make the right financial decisions. This lack of financial confidence could affect your children's confidence in other areas of their lives.

DANGER 5

The Apple Doesn't Fall Far from the Tree

Although you want to take an active role in teaching your kids about money, you could teach them the wrong things. For example, you might use money to motivate your kids to score goals or get better report cards. These bribes (which are discussed in Chapter 2: Tricks or Treats) can teach your kids to equate money with success; that money is the only real reward for an achievement. In this way, you might teach your kids the wrong values even when you have all the best intentions. That's why this book stresses the importance of "principles." You and your children need to think about your money principles before you take action. By observing the principles, you'll be less likely to do the wrong thing.

DANGER 6

Family Conflict

You could wreck your family relationships because of conflicts related to money. In my opinion this danger is the most serious. It is not uncommon for families to be torn apart by disputes over business and inheritances. Even when the sums are modest, money-related tensions can arise. This tension between spouses and parents and their children can destroy the love and joy that should be a part of marriage and family life. If you don't have strong principles, and a plan of action, your relationship with your kids could be consumed with arguments over allowance and other financial issues.

Since I started developing The Making Allowances

System, I've noticed that most parents feel threatened by these dangers — either because they did nothing to teach their kids about money, or because they thought their own good financial habits would somehow rub off on their kids. For the most part, we parents lack the knowledge, structure and tools to teach our kids helpful money management skills. This book was written to help you avoid these dangers.

Kids and Money: The Opportunities

On the positive side of the ledger, this book will help you take advantage of the many opportunities you have to teach your kids about money. The opportunities are legion, but six major ones stand out.

OPPORTUNITY 1

Your Kids can Become Financially Responsible Adults

If you help your kids develop good money habits when they're young, they will have a better chance of being successful as adults. They'll learn to make choices, become more independent and will know how to set and achieve financial goals.

OPPORTUNITY 2

Your Kids can Develop Strong Positive Values about Money

You have an opportunity to help your kids develop a good attitude towards money; that money is not an end in itself, but a means to achieve more important goals in their life. They can develop a sense of self worth that's not tied to the size of their bank account, nor to the kind of running shoes they wear. As well, if they develop a good attitude toward money, they may be better able to resist the negative aspects of peer pressure.

Your Kids will Learn Consistent Money Habits and Useful Financial Skills

With your help, your kids can grow up knowing how to set financial goals, how to follow a budget and how to handle money on a daily basis. They will also learn to save money regularly, make smart buying decisions, and set their own priorities on spending.

Your Kids will Develop the Confidence to Make their Own Choices

By teaching your kids how to handle their own money from an early age, you will give them increasing confidence to make their own choices. They won't feel they always need to turn to you and other people to make decisions for them. If they develop confidence about money early on, they will be better able to handle increasing responsibility as they get older. As well, their confidence about money will translate into confidence about other areas of their life, such as school, athletics, personal relationships and community involvement.

You can Teach your Kids the Right Things about Money

If you adhere to the proven process in this book, you'll become more confident about teaching your kids. You will see the results throughout their childhood and teens. You'll know you're teaching the right principles the right way. (That's not to say you'll agree with everything I say in this book, but it will help you decide what's right for you, and that will further increase your confidence.)

OPPORTUNITY 6

You can Improve your Relationship with your Kids by Teaching them about Money

As you work with your kids on the concepts, you have the opportunity to discuss thousands of topics. That's because money issues affect virtually every area of our lives. As you progress, you'll learn a lot about your kids, and they'll learn a lot about you. You'll also work as a team, instead of as adversaries. This chance to be a team is, in my mind, the greatest opportunity of all.

The Making Allowances System

Helping you avoid these dangers and realise these opportunities is the purpose behind The Making Allowances System. It provides the principles, structure and tools you need to teach your kids about money. The system is presented Step-by-Step as a series of distinct concepts (one per chapter) to help support you in your knowledge of money management. Each concept contains four primary components:

Slice of Life

Do you have a dating teenager in your home? It is always interesting to talk about what they are spending on their dating relationship. Do they expect to pay only for themselves? Are expensive gifts essential on special occasions? You might be surprised by their ideas on this subject.

1. Achievable Goals

For each concept, I provide three goals to achieve along with a time estimate of how long it should take your family to master these goals. All of the principles, structures and tools presented in each chapter are designed to help you achieve these goals.

2. Guiding Principles

I present the basic principles of how best to teach your kids each concept. Learning the principles first will give you more confidence when you are teaching your kids. It will also make it easier for your kids to understand why you want them to do things a certain way. Build upon what you are doing well and what you see will be best for each of your children.

3. A Step-by-Step System

Lack of structure is one major weakness of most kids and money books. They contain a lot of useful information, but they don't give you any real ideas about how to put this information into action. The Making Allowances System is different. For each concept, I conclude the chapter by giving you a Step-by-Step system to follow. This structure will bolster your confidence, and help your kids learn faster and more effectively. Some chapters, particularly the first six, need to be completed before moving onto the later chapters, and some will follow along as slowly or quickly as your family dictates.

4. Skillsheets, Tips and Traps, and Practical Examples

To help you teach your kids important money concepts, and to keep everyone on track, I've provided some practical tools such as skillsheets for your family to work on together (available in this book

and on our website www.makingallowances.com).
I've also added lots of take-action tips. In addition,
I share some kids and money stories from my own
life and from the experiences of other people, some
real-life, "Slices of Life."

Before reading this book, you should know that I, in an
attempt to be gender neutral, alternate between the use
of "he" and "she," "his" and "her." However, I make
no effort to use feminine and masculine pronouns in
precisely equal numbers. "Any child is every child, and
it is children who are important" (Jean Ross Peterson).

So What About You?

One thing I've learned about parents: they can often
be very hard on themselves. They worry they're not
doing the right things, that they're not spending
enough time with their kids, that they're too strict or
too lax. No matter what they do, they don't think it's
enough. Well, if you're in this camp, I'm here to tell
you that things aren't as bad as they seem. If you have
kids of school age, you owe yourself a pat on the back.
You've managed the following:

- You've got children. This is a major achievement in
  itself because you've accepted the responsibility of
  being a parent, and you've made a huge commitment.
- You love your kids. You wouldn't be reading this
  book if you didn't. You provide a caring, nurturing
  environment for your kids.
- You've helped them develop some important skills
  and habits.
- You've probably started some kind of money program with your kids (allowance, regular savings,
  bank accounts) and you've established some poli-
  cies about chores and treats.

- You've worked on your own personal financial habits. You may have an RRSP, a regular savings plan, an education savings plan, an investment portfolio and other cornerstones of sound financial planning (i.e. wills and insurance).
- You bought this book. That statement might sound self-serving coming from the author, but the fact you bought this book indicates you care a lot about your kids' future.

So there you go. Things are a lot better than you might think. All of these accomplishments are the stepping stones to your next stage as a parent: beginning to teach your kids about the world of money. You are ready to begin using The Making Allowances System.

Just a Little About Me

So why am I qualified to write this book? Well, first of all, I'm a parent myself. I've been using this system with my three boys — Ryan, Patrick and Jeremy — for more than 10 years. I've proven it works with my kids (they've become financially mature teenagers), and with many other parents and their kids.

In addition to my qualifications as a parent, I'm also a professional financial planner with more than 15 years of experience. As I mentioned earlier, I've worked with hundreds of individuals and couples, most of whom are parents. I've learned first-hand their own problems, and the challenges they face teaching their kids about money.

But most of all, I'm qualified to help you teach your kids because I am passionate about helping parents and their kids learn money management skills. I've developed and tested every principle because I believe everyone can benefit from these skills. The system works and I want to share with you the same good experience I've had with my kids. So I hope you'll join me on this exciting adventure.

The Universal Principles

In each chapter, I provide several key principles to help you teach and implement each concept. These sub-principles are based on a number of universal principles which you should understand right from the start. These principles are:

UNIVERSAL PRINCIPLE 1
Talk About It

Maintaining an on-going dialogue with your kids is the best way to teach them about money. Whenever you introduce a new concept, or face a showdown over a money-related issue, the most effective way to address it is to talk about it. Choosing an appropriate time to talk is also important.

UNIVERSAL PRINCIPLE 2
Start Early

Ideally, start working with your children at an early age, preferably age five or six. If you wait until your kids are in their teens, it will be more difficult, (but not impossible) to teach them new money principles and concepts. Stick to the system presented in this book to bring your teens to the skill level they need.

UNIVERSAL PRINCIPLE 3
Give Up Control

To learn about money, your kids have to do things themselves. Instead of handling their money for them, let them do it. Let them make deposits and withdrawals from the bank; let them make their own purchases; let them decide what they want to buy with their own money. You can offer advice, but let them do it on their own. It's the best way to learn any new skill.

UNIVERSAL PRINCIPLE 4
Let your Kids Make Mistakes

Even if you think your kids are spending their allowance on the wrong things, let them do it. Don't intervene and take charge. Let them make mistakes. If they mess up, they'll learn the lesson much faster than by listening to a lecture. Making inexpensive mistakes when you are a child and learning from them is far better than making costly mistakes as an adult.

UNIVERSAL PRINCIPLE 5
Set Limits

Although you need to give your kids money for allowance, for treats on special occasions, and for the purchase of "cool" clothes and other stuff, you have to set limits. You have to teach your kids that money doesn't come pouring out of bank machines. They have to learn to make choices based on financial limits. Even if you have a large income, and lots of money to spend on your kids, they will learn to manage money well only if they operate within some kind of set budget. So set limits.

UNIVERSAL PRINCIPLE 6
Provide Structure

As a parent, it's your job to help your kids express their individuality and creativity within a well-defined structure. This is especially important when you teach your kids about money. You need to help them establish a consistent regime of allowance, saving and spending. This type of structure will help them learn faster and with more confidence.

How to Make Allowances

As you work through The Making Allowances System with your kids, keep a sense of humour. When the unexpected happens — and it will — go with the flow. Improvise. Let your kids make mistakes. Let yourself make mistakes. Make allowances. Most of all, enjoy your relationships with your children.

Share Your Stories

I hope you and your children enjoy this book. I invite your feedback, advice, and personal stories on the Making Allowances Official Kids and Parents website at www.makingallowances.com. You can also e-mail me at makingallowances@ifc.fpc.ca.

Just Begin

As you read, take note of the ideas that particularly grab you. What ideas make sense to you, and seem reasonable to try in your family? You may want to implement the concepts slowly, and limit yourself to one concept per month. Or perhaps you have teenagers, and feel the need to jump in and implement many concepts at once. Whatever your situation, there is help to be had. And remember, you must make allowances for yourself too — you will make mistakes, or handle a situation badly, but you can always start afresh. And you may find that some of the concepts will not work well for you, or may not apply to your particular situation. The important thing is for you and your children to talk about money and learn how to manage it — both independently, and together. I am excited about the adventure before you, and wish you well as you begin to "make allowances."

CHAPTER 1

The Allowance Contract

3 MAJOR GOALS

TIME TO IMPLEMENT: One to six months

1 To introduce your children to the value of money

2 To teach your children the basics of good money management

3 To begin a lifelong habit of saving money

When your child reaches the age of five or six, it's time for you to introduce her to the world of money. By this age, she will be familiar with money on several levels — she can count it, identify the different denominations and recognise that she needs a specific amount to buy the goods she wants. Thus it is a natural time to establish an allowance system. Some children may be ready at a younger age, especially if they are avid counters, or shoppers. But I would urge you not to rush your children. Pre-schoolers can be given change to put in the piggybank, or helped to roll pennies, or purchase a candy bar, but an allowance is not necessary.

The first step is to establish an allowance program. This may sound like a simple matter, but it isn't always. You may wonder:

- Should I give my child an allowance at all?
- If so, how much money should I give?
- When should I give it?
- What should the allowance be used for?
- If I give my child an allowance, who pays for special treats?
- Should my child earn the allowance by doing chores around the house?
- Should the allowance be tied to achievement at school, or used to encourage good behaviour?
- Should part of the money be put in the bank as savings?

In most cases, parents answer their questions about allowances by drawing on their own experiences. They say: "When I was her age, I got 25 cents a week for allowance, and it was plenty." Or they say: "I didn't get any allowance; I had to earn money by doing chores around the house." Looking around, parents also consider examples set by relatives, friends and neighbours. They say: "His cousin gets an allowance of $20 a month, so that's what we'll do." Or they say: "Suzie across the street only gets an allowance if she makes her bed every day."

Unfortunately, taking your lead from the past, or from people around you, is a strategy fraught with peril. What worked 25 years ago probably won't fly today. The world, and kids, have changed dramatically since you were growing up. Today we are bombarded with more advertising, more choice of products and many of us have a busier, more stressful lifestyle than our parents did. In the same way, what appears to work across the street might be the wrong approach in your house. Every family has different values, customs, income levels and attitudes towards money.

So what can you do when faced with all these divergent examples? It's quite simple, really. Create your approach based on certain principles which have been proven to work over and over again, by my own family and by the families of many of my clients and friends. I call these, "The Key Allowance Principles."

The Key Allowance Principles

Allowance Principle 1: **Make a promise to your child.**

Allowance Principle 2: **Have your child make a promise to you.**

Allowance Principle 3: **Be consistent and firm.**

Allowance Principle 4: **Don't tie allowance to chores or achievement.**

Allowance Principle 5: **Make savings part of the allowance contract.**

ALLOWANCE PRINCIPLE 1

Make a Promise to Your Child

You may choose to give the first allowance as a significant rite of passage. "When you are five (or six ... or
whatever age you decide) you are entitled to an
allowance." This approach is helpful in families with
several children because young children have something to look forward to. Explain to your child that an
allowance is a set amount of money, given weekly, to
enable them to pay for things that are important to
them, such as toys or candy or books.

Before you start your allowance system, promise your
child a specific amount of money on a specific day of
every week. Give an amount you deem appropriate.
My guideline is one dollar times half their age, per
week. (I handle this suggestion in greater detail later in
the chapter.) Establish a day of the week, such as
Sunday or Monday, which makes sense for your family situation. Of course, the point of making the
promise is that you keep it.

ALLOWANCE PRINCIPLE 2

Have Your Child Make a Promise to You

Before she receives the allowance, suggest that your
child promise you two things. One, she will save part
of the allowance for savings. Two, the rest of her
money will be mad money — used for fun — and she
won't nag you for more when it's all gone. If she does
not have enough money to buy everything she wants,
she can do extra odd jobs around the house for payment, or try to find small jobs to do around the neighbourhood.

ALLOWANCE PRINCIPLE 3
Be Consistent and Firm

Once you start giving your child an allowance, try to be consistent, and give the amount of money you promised, on the day you promised. Remember your child looks forward to that allowance the same way you anticipate your pay cheque. If your child spends his allowance right away, don't top it up! Tell your child he will have to wait until the next allowance day. You may hear nagging and whining and even slamming of doors once in a while, but it won't go on year after year — your child will know the buck stops there! If your child thinks you will always give more money if it runs out, he will never learn to manage the allowance.

ALLOWANCE PRINCIPLE 4
Don't Tie Allowance to Chores or Achievement

A child should receive an allowance for being part of a family. In my experience, and according to many psychologists and counsellors, an allowance should not be tied to personal achievement such as getting an A on a report card, or doing chores around the house. (See Chapter 2 for more discussion on this issue.) Encourage hard work and good behaviour, and reward achievement in other meaningful ways. In other words, do not use allowance as a bribe or a reward. Give an allowance to teach your children the basics of good money management.

ALLOWANCE PRINCIPLE 5

Make Savings Part of the Allowance Contract

Saving money is a habit that should be learned at an early age. The best time to begin teaching this habit is the first time you give your child an allowance. I suggest you require your child to save 25 per cent of their allowance each week, and put the savings in the bank, or piggy bank, every month. Help them set a goal for something they would like to buy with the savings. Ask them to agree to keep the savings for the first three months, to build patience and a larger savings amount.

In my experience, these five allowance principles are very important. Over the last 10 years, our children — who are currently 15, 13, and 11 — have had their own money to spend on treats, purchased CD players with their own savings, saved travel money, given to charity and put long-term savings into mutual funds. We have used these allowance principles to teach our children good money management skills. If you incorporate these principles into your routines, your child will learn valuable lessons about money, and develop skills and habits that will last a lifetime.

Making Allowances for the First Time

To reflect the five allowance principles, I created The Allowance Contract, which you can use to set up an allowance program with your child. It's a step-by-step process that has worked in my family, and in hundreds of other families.

After reading Chapters 1, 2 and 3, sit down with your younger children and go over the Allowance Contract (see Skillsheet 1.1). Explain to them that a contract is a promise or agreement to do something. Give them an opportunity to ask questions, and bring up questions if your children don't. The important thing is to get them thinking about money and how to handle it.

For older children 12 and up, also read Chapter 4, and then share the concepts with them. You may even want to read parts of the chapters together. Don't skip steps. Remember: these are habit-forming life skills that will impact your children for a lifetime. Your goal in giving an allowance is to create money-smart kids who are able to spend, save and make good consumer decisions at all stages of life.

The Amount and the Day

The first step in the process is to determine the amount of the allowance, and the day of the week for giving it. Give careful consideration to choosing the amount. One guideline would be to give an amount equal to half the age of the child (e.g. a 10-year-old would receive $5 a week). Another option is to give a dollar amount per the age of the child (e.g. $10 a week for a 10-year-old). Realistically, the amount you decide on will depend on your financial situation. Decide on an amount you know you can pay out every week, and that will give your child a reasonable amount of savings and weekly spending money.

Give the allowance in coins, especially to young children. This will help them to better understand the amount of money they are receiving (and gives them practical math skills, too). In addition, coins can easily be divided into amounts for the piggy bank and the wallet. Handling money each week will build good, practical habits for the future.

I also recommend you give the allowance on Sunday night or on Monday. If you give it on Friday, all of it is bound to disappear over the weekend.

How much is enough? I have found that an amount of half the age of the child works well for most families. This amount gives them some spending money, and leaves enough to save to make average purchases over a month or two. An average purchase for a six-year-old might be a small toy or book. A 10-year-old might purchase a CD or toy. A 14-year-old might buy clothing or a video game. Also, it is not so much that they can buy whatever they want. They are still motivated to do odd jobs or look for ways to earn money, especially as they get older and their interests and hobbies often become much more expensive. Cash and gift certificates are often given as gifts these days, so the child usually has another source of savings that can be added to the allowance.

Savings for the Future
Figure out how much you want your child to save. I recommend 25 per cent, but you can go higher or lower. Financial experts often suggest that adults set aside a minimum of 10 per cent of their income for savings. If we can start our kids with a higher ideal, when they are older they will see 10 per cent as an easy goal to attain. Teaching children to save will help them to become good financial managers and become financially independent. This, in turn, will help you, the parent, put away your long-term savings because you will not have to fund the lifestyle of your young adult!

Sometimes, the child wants to try and save more than 25 per cent, but saving too much money can pose a problem. If the remaining money isn't adequate to cover those trips to the corner store, your child will be tempted to raid the piggybank and upset the savings plan, or come to you for more money.

Get a Piggybank and Wallet

Go out with your child and buy the kind of piggybank you can open without breaking, and a wallet. For young children four and up it is especially important for them to handle the money. The piggybank is for their savings, and the wallet is for their spending money. Having both gives the child a concrete understanding of the two concepts, saving and spending. If you have children over 10, a bank account can take the place of the piggybank.

As soon as you give the allowance to your child, have him or her put the savings portion into the piggybank. At the end of the month, you can go to the bank, set up an account, and deposit the accumulated savings. As agreed, the savings will not be withdrawn for three months, in order to allow a large amount to build. After the three-month start-up period, the savings can be withdrawn at any time to purchase the items listed in the contract. (Using this saving method is good training for preventing impulse buying!)

The Allowance Contract

Creating The Allowance Contract is the next step in the process. Before you give your child the allowance, sit down together and work out a simple contract. In the contract, you promise to give a set amount of allowance on a given day of the week. In return, your child promises to:

- save 25 per cent of the allowance;
- put the savings in the bank at the end of the month;
- not withdraw savings from the bank for the first three months;
- spend the savings on items related to the goals your child set.

The Allowance Contract

Skillsheet 1.1

(Child) I, _____ will:

- receive $ _____ allowance every Sunday/Monday
- put _____% of allowance away for savings
- visit the bank on the last Saturday of every month to deposit savings
- retrieve savings only after it reaches a minimum of $ _____
- supply an outline of what allowance and savings will be used for

(Parent) I, _____ will:

- pay $ _____ allowance every Sunday/Monday
- receive an outline of what allowance will be used for
- receive an outline of what savings will be used for: short and long term

I, _____ will use my allowance for the following:

-
-
-
-
-

I, _____ will use my savings for the following:

-
-
-
-
-

_____   _____
Child   Parent

_____   _____
Date   Date

Committing to these promises teaches your child about developing good financial habits, setting goals and making a commitment. Making the allowance contract is a lot of fun, and gives your child the opportunity to ask lots of questions about money. You'll be surprised at the questions children ask!

You can use our ready-made Allowance Contract at Skillsheet 1.1, download a copy free from www.makingallowances.com on the Web or put together your own contract.

The Allowance Tracker

To help you be consistent in your allowance program, I suggest you keep a written record of the allowance you have given out. This has been one of the most important forms for our family because it is a visual reminder that the allowance has been paid. A copy of this valuable form can be found at Skillsheet 1.2.

Let's say that your usual night to give out allowances is Monday, and you realise at 9:00 PM that not only have you forgotten to pay, but you don't have the correct change in your wallet. It's late, it's raining, and you decide to pay the allowance on Tuesday instead. Then, before you know it, it's Friday, and you can't remember if you paid the allowance this week or not. Keeping a record enables you to figure out when you last paid, and how much. In addition, when your child comes to you to nag about not having received their allowance, "for at least three weeks!" you can pull out your proof and the discussion is over. You'll either have to apologise and pay out, or smile smugly.

I find this tracking method especially helpful if there are multiple children in the family or if you have a shared parenting arrangement.

Allowance Tracker

Skillsheet 1.2

Date	Child #1	Child #2	Child #3
January			
Week #1			
Week #2			
Week #3			
Week #4			
Week #5			
Other Job(s)			
February			
Week #1			
Week #2			
Week #3			
Week #4			
Week #5			
Other Job(s)			
March			
Week #1			
Week #2			
Week #3			
Week #4			
Week #5			
Other Job(s)			
April			
Week #1			
Week #2			
Week #3			
Week #4			
Week #5			
Other Job(s)			

Allowance Tracker (cont'd)

Date	Child #1	Child #2	Child #3
May			
Week #1			
Week #2			
Week #3			
Week #4			
Week #5			
Other Job(s)			
June			
Week #1			
Week #2			
Week #3			
Week #4			
Week #5			
Other Job(s)			
July			
Week #1			
Week #2			
Week #3			
Week #4			
Week #5			
Other Job(s)			
August			
Week #1			
Week #2			
Week #3			
Week #4			
Week #5			
Other Job(s)			

Allowance Tracker (cont'd)

Date	Child #1	Child #2	Child #3
September			
Week #1			
Week #2			
Week #3			
Week #4			
Week #5			
Other Job(s)			
October			
Week #1			
Week #2			
Week #3			
Week #4			
Week #5			
Other Job(s)			
November			
Week #1			
Week #2			
Week #3			
Week #4			
Week #5			
Other Job(s)			
December			
Week #1			
Week #2			
Week #3			
Week #4			
Week #5			
Other Job(s)			

Deliver Yourself from Temptation

It may be hard, but don't relent when your child asks for more money. Your child has to learn that money does not come free from the bank machine, in endless amounts. Be consistent. Stick to the allowance contract.

The Step-by-Step System

1 Decide on the specific amount for the allowance.

2 Decide the day of week to give the allowance.

3 Decide on the savings amount (25 per cent recommended).

4 Have a wallet and piggybank for your child.

5 Talk to your child, and explain the allowance contract.

6 Prepare the contract together and sign it.

7 Give the allowance on a pre-determined day (in coins).

8 Have your child put savings (25 per cent) in the piggybank.

9 Have your child put the rest of allowance in the wallet.

10 At the end of the month, put the accumulated savings into the bank.

CHAPTER 2

Tricks or Treats?

3 MAJOR GOALS

TIME TO IMPLEMENT: One to three months

1 To learn the difference between allowance, treats, and family expenditures

2 To give treats without negatively affecting good allowance habits

3 To teach your children about generosity, sharing, and appreciation

When you and your children have established a regular allowance plan, it's time to work on the next major issue faced by parents about kids and money: treats.

If you give your children $5 or $10 in allowance every Sunday night, you might ask yourself: "Why should I treat my kids to special snacks or outings if I already give them money every week?" Or, "Why should I reward my children for their good report cards if I give them an allowance?" And what about regular outings to movies, football games, or concerts? Are these considered treats or something else? "Should my kids be required to pay for their own entertainment tickets out of their allowance?"

Allowance, Treats or Family Expenditures?

The difference between these three concepts — allowance, treats and regular family expenditures — can get blurred, especially in your child's mind, and this ambiguity can undermine the good habits you're trying to instil with the Allowance Contract. So it's important to make the distinctions between the concepts as clear as possible. I have found it best to distinguish them this way:

An allowance is given to a child on a regular, consistent basis. In simple terms, a child should receive his allowance for simply being a member of the family, in order to instil good money management skills. It is used by the child when he wishes to spend his money on an item for himself or for others. It's not given as a treat or as a reward, nor is it taken away as a punishment. The money should not be used to pay for family outings, unless these outings are the idea of the child — a movie, for example. In our family, when the kids ask to go out for a fast food lunch, we offer to drive, if they pay for their own lunch.

Treats are given by parents to model positive values such as generosity, sharing, togetherness, fun and appreciation. Treats can be given spontaneously, such as when you've been at a baseball practice, and decide to pull into a corner store to buy everyone a cold drink. Or, treats can be planned: for example, when you take a child on a monthly "date," or perhaps you develop a tradition of taking the kids out for breakfast on the first day of school. Finally, treats can be given as a reward for the achievement of a goal. You may take your honour role student out for a special lunch, or buy your swimmer a new bathing suit when he beats his personal best.

We had a reluctant reader at our house, and found that if we rewarded him with a new book when he finished reading one, he became excited about reading. He is now a voracious reader, and the added bonus is that his school grades have improved. Most counsellors and child specialists believe it is better to give a reward with something tangible than to give money. Money is a commodity of exchange and is not an exchange of value or worth. Don't let your child equate her self-esteem and worth to the amount of money she receives!

Family expenditures are made on a regular basis, and are paid for by the parents. For example, the family might buy pizza on Friday nights, or go bowling every Saturday afternoon. The child is not required to contribute part of his allowance. Like allowance, the benefits of these expenditures are given for simply being a member of the family.

| Slice of Life | When our family goes on long road trips, we provide the meals, and the children pay for their own treats. Decide on what guidelines will work for your family, discuss them with your children and then stick with them! |

The Key Treats Principles

Treats Principle 1: **Make a distinction between allowance and treats.**

Treats Principle 2: **Make the distinction between treats and family expenditures.**

Treats Principle 3: **Give treats to model positive values.**

Treats Principle 4: **Give treats to encourage positive lifestyle choices.**

Treats Principle 5: **Don't try to create the perfect balance among siblings.**

TREATS PRINCIPLE 1

Make a Distinction Between Allowance and Treats

As I've said, you need to communicate clearly to your child the difference between when you expect her to use her allowance and when you will be paying for treats. Review the Allowance Contract with your child and go over again what she can buy with her allowance. Talk about other things you might buy as a treat. Create a list of treats with your child and then discuss reasons why you would give her a treat:

- As a Reward: for a good report card, passing a grade, achieving a goal, good behaviour and helpfulness; or

- Spontaneously: on the spur of the moment to express affection, appreciation and generosity. Decide if treats should include shopping for larger items such as clothes, or only include shopping for small inexpensive items.

TREATS PRINCIPLE 2

Make the Distinction Between Treats and Family Expenditures

Speak to your child about the difference between a treat (given as a spontaneous reward or planned), and a regular family expenditure such as a weekly chocolate bar or trips to the zoo. Create another list of family expenditures. Explain that she does not need to contribute to these family expenditures.

TREATS PRINCIPLE 3

Give Treats to Model Positive Values

When treats are given as a reward, they teach your child such values as hard work, achievement, and appreciation. When treats are given spontaneously, they teach your child about generosity, sharing and togetherness. Treats also teach your kids how to say "please" and "thank you," and provide a model for the important principle of "share the wealth" when we have an abundance of good fortune.

TREATS PRINCIPLE 4

Give Treats to Encourage Positive Lifestyle Choices

Treats do not have to come in the form of candy, fast food, or a trip to the arcade. While your child may ask you for these things, you can choose other treats which you consider more positive, such as educational toys, books, or tickets to a classical music concert, play or sporting event.

TREATS PRINCIPLE 5

Don't Try to Create the Perfect Balance Among Siblings

If you have two or more children, doling out treats can cause a serious outbreak of sibling rivalry. When one child is given a treat, the other child may feel he is falling behind in the great "treat" register in the sky. If this happens, don't try to level the playing field. Children have to learn that life is not about making everything come out evenly. Sometimes there is an imbalance, but that's the way it goes. This is normal! Don't get mad when your kids cry or yell or get mad at you. Help them understand. If you give in, and try to even the score, your children will begin to view treats as a "right" rather than something that is given or received as a privilege.

The problem of sibling rivalry is especially difficult when you have children with large gaps between ages. For example, you might give your 16-year-old a $150 track suit, and your 9-year-old a $25 T-shirt. There is a vast difference in the money spent, but your 9-year-old should not expect you to spend $150 on him or her as well. So don't try to even the score. Give treats when and how you see fit. But be consistent so as not to play favourites. Parents need to be on side with one another to keep a balance.

Slice of Life — When our family goes out to the movies as a family event, we parents make a family expenditure. If one of the children wishes to go with a friend to a movie, he must use some of his own allowance. Younger children can pay a portion, and teens can pay for the ticket on their own — especially if they are working.

The Treats Planner

Giving treats to your children can be one of the greatest pleasures in life. It's satisfying to see them break into a wide grin with a sparkle in their eyes when you give them a treat. The trick, as I've said, is to keep treats separate from allowance and family expenditures. It's also important not to spoil your kids. Otherwise, they will come to expect treats on a regular basis and won't appreciate them.

You can create a Treats Planner* skillsheet and use it to keep track of all of the treats you give to your kids, what you bought, where you bought it, and how much you spent. You should also keep track of why you gave them the treat, and their reaction to it. This can be used to see your patterns of giving treats or to solve a problem. For example, perhaps one of your children is more demanding or insistent than the others, and seems to get more than her fair share of treats. You can use a Treats Planner to monitor the situation. You may decide it is best not to share this information with your children.

A Treats Planner is not meant to take the fun and spontaneity out of giving treats. It's designed to help you and your kids keep track of what you are doing,

---

 Slice of Life	I had the boys help do a spring clean-up of the deck. It was a time-consuming, tiresome job that the kids grumbled through. After they completed the job, I took them to a favourite ice cream store as a reward for sticking with it (but made no mention of the possibility of a treat beforehand).

---

*I have created a Treats Planner Skillsheet and it is available at www.makingallowances.com.

and to identify ways to improve the process. In fact, it's only meant to be used for a brief time. Once you and your children have developed your own way of handling treats, you will no longer need the form.

Treats Tips & Traps

1 If your child does not appreciate a treat: If your child doesn't appreciate the treat, don't scold him, or vow to cut out treats altogether. At a later time, speak to your child about what happened. Express your disappointment in his behaviour. Explain that a treat is to be appreciated, and you wish to receive a polite expression of gratitude when you give a treat.

2 Don't give money as a reward: I recommend you don't give your child money as a reward for an achievement. Give him or her something more meaningful such as an educational toy, books, trips to sports or cultural events.

3 Let your kids decide on their own rewards: If you want to motivate your child, let him or her decide on the treat they want as a reward. Of course, you can help with ideas, and set a reasonable budget, but from my experience, children get more excited about a treat they've chosen, rather than one decided on by a parent.

4 How to handle birthdays and special holidays: Special days such as birthdays, Christmas or Hanukkah can turn into an avalanche of gift giving. At a time when your kids are getting lots of presents and special treats from their relatives, it's important for you to make a clear distinction about a special treat. If you are going to give an additional treat over a holiday, communicate as clearly as possible the reason that you are providing the treat. Note: I find it is during these special occasions that I worry the most about spoiling my children. It is helpful to have a budgeted amount to keep within the boundaries of our own cash management.

5 How to handle the generous relative: Your child may have a relative who loves to lavish treats and presents on them. While this generosity is wonderful on one hand, it can raise the expectations of your child much higher than you want. If this happens, I suggest you talk to the relative about the issue, and see if they can bring their generosity more in line with your own. If they continue to load on the treats, you will need to speak with your children, and explain that the relative's style of giving treats is different from your own.

These are a few examples of issues we parents have to wrestle with. Use our email address to share with us or ask questions (makingallowances@ifc.fpc.ca).

The Step-by-Step System

1 Discuss with your spouse the difference between allowances, treats and family expenditures.

2 Decide what is to be included in the categories.

3 Decide when treats, allowances and family expenditures will be given.

4 Go over the Allowance Contract with your children. Discuss what treats they will buy and how much money they are to save.

5 Discuss with your children some ideas for treats and family expenditures.

6 Discuss with your children how treats may differ between them, based on age and interests.

CHAPTER 3

Laughing All the Way to the Bank

---
3 MAJOR GOALS

TIME TO IMPLEMENT: Two to three months

1 To teach your children how to save money regularly

2 To teach your children about banks and how they work

3 To teach your children how to deal with people with regard to money matters

Many adults don't know how to handle money properly because they didn't handle money enough when they were children. Instead their parents did all of the spending, banking and saving. If you want your children to grow up to be financially responsible adults, I believe you have to let them handle money often. At an early age, they need to learn how banks work and why it's important to deposit money in a bank on a regular basis. They also need to develop the habit of saving money for larger purchases. (In Chapter 9, we will talk about investing and long-term savings.) These lessons will help your children develop a much more comprehensive understanding of money and how to manage it.

The Key Banking Principles

Banking Principle 1: **Make regular savings a lifelong habit.**

Banking Principle 2: **Let the child do it.**

Banking Principle 3: **Don't pass on the passbook**

Banking Principle 4: **Just say no to bank cards.**

Banking Principle 5: **Set a maximum limit on spending money.**

Banking Principle 6: **Flee from dreaded bank fees.**

Banking Principle 7: **Put little interest in interest.**

BANKING PRINCIPLE 1
Make Regular Savings a Lifelong Habit

In Chapter 1 The Allowance Contract, you set up a weekly allowance routine with your children. If you have been following the system, your children have been saving a set percentage of their allowance in their piggy banks. This money should be put in a child's savings account. Plan to set up the account to make regular deposits of these savings, about once a month. Whatever age you may start this with your child, it is good for them to get comfortable going to the bank and understanding it is an institution that can help them when used properly.

BANKING PRINCIPLE 2
Let the Child Do It

Let your child make withdrawals on and deposits to his bank account. Let him fill out the deposit/withdrawal slips, stand in line, and count the money (with your help). Older children will be able to use the bank machine later but it's important that your child first learn to deal directly with the tellers. Your child needs to develop skills to negotiate money matters directly with people, not machines! Later in life they will still have to negotiate car loans, mortgages, and business financing with people. This step is important to build your child's confidence.

BANKING PRINCIPLE 3
Don't Pass on the Passbook

When you go to the bank to set up an account with your child, get a passbook. (Some banks give you the option of a passbook or a monthly statement.) With a passbook, your child will be able to see every deposit and withdrawal at the moment they happen, and be

Slice of Life

Even with my boys at 15, 13 and 11, an upper limit of about $20 stands, due to wallets that get lost, money that disappears at school or when friends have been over, and when shopping, especially for teens, because of the potential for being mugged, or as teens call it, "jacked."

holding something that feels real. This experience will heighten his awareness of the banking process.

BANKING PRINCIPLE 4

Just Say No to Bank Cards

When you set up your child's bank account, the bank will offer you a bank card. I advise you against accepting it. Young children are not ready to use a bank card. They need to understand and be able to handle money in a practical way before advancing to the electronic system.

Bank cards allow children to make transactions without knowing where the money is coming from. For example, when Jeremy was six years old, I told him I didn't have any money in my wallet for McDonald's, so he told me to get the "free money" from the bank machine!

Bank cards make children's savings too readily available, and they will nickel and dime their savings to nothing. A bank card will also undermine the good savings habits you are trying to foster. Note: bank cards should be introduced to your children when they are in their early teens. (See Chapter 8.)

BANKING PRINCIPLE 5

Set a Maximum Limit on Spending Money

Even though your child deposits savings in the bank, she may accumulate additional money by saving her spending money as well as gift money. If the amount of money in her wallet gets too large, she should put the excess into the bank as well. I recommend you set an upper limit in her wallet of about $20 or two weeks allowance. This amount will be enough money so they can buy some fairly nice items without needing to make a withdrawal from the bank.

| BANKING PRINCIPLE 6 |
Flee from Dreaded Bank Fees

Most banks have special savings accounts for children. These accounts usually have no bank fees. So make sure you open a child account. If you use a regular adult account, the bank fees could quickly erode the small amount saved by your children. (Learning about bank fees is an important lesson, but not one your child needs to learn at this point.)

| BANKING PRINCIPLE 7 |
Put Little Interest in Interest

When I was a child, interest rates on savings accounts were much higher than today. If I received 50 cents in interest, I could spend that money on something substantial. Today, however, interest rates are much lower, and you can't buy much with 50 cents anymore. So don't make a big deal about the interest earned on your child's account. At this point the important thing is helping them to make regular savings, and build good habits.

The Kid's Bank Money Tracker

Although your child will receive a passbook when you open up the account, it may be important that he keep his own separate records of the deposits and withdrawals, just as you do with your own ledger or computer accounting program.

---

*I have created a Kid's Bank Money Tracker and it is available at www.makingallowances.com.

To help you, develop a Kid's Bank Money Tracker*
skillsheet. The form can be a simple ledger to keep
track of deposits and withdrawals, and of course, the
balance in the account.

Banking Tips & Traps

1 Making the bank appointment: Before going
to the bank to set up your kids' accounts, call
the branch and make an appointment. Tell
them you are bringing your children and
would like to meet with a representative who
is good with kids.

2 Keeping the passbook safe: As I suggest for
your child's wallet, establish a regular, safe
place to keep the passbook to avoid losing it.
I suggest you keep the passbook yourself, and
give it to your kids when they make deposits
or withdrawals.

The Step-by-Step System

1 **Discuss with Your Child the Reasons to
Open a Bank Account**
These reasons include to:
- save money for large purchases in the
future
- keep money safe from loss or theft
- give you access to your money when
you need it, where you need it

- earn money on their savings through interest
- save money for holidays

2 **Set Up a Bank Account**

Go with your child to your local bank branch to open up a bank account. Take the piggy bank, or if the child has a large amount of coins, help her count and roll out the coins at home. When you open the account, make sure it's a no-fee children's account. Have the bank representative explain the whole process to your child, and have her sign the forms. It's a great experience for your child.

3 **Make the First Deposit**

When you open up the account, deposit the money from the piggy bank. Help your child fill out the deposit slips. When you get the passbook back, look it over with your child. Make deposits on a regular basis; I suggest monthly.

4 **4 Have Your Child Keep their Own Records**

Create a Kid's Bank Money Tracker skillsheet or print out a copy from our website.

CHAPTER 4

Spending the Bigger Bucks

3 MAJOR GOALS

TIME TO IMPLEMENT: Two to three months

1 To teach your children how to be good consumers

2 To teach your children how to make wise buying decisions

3 To teach your children the relationship between price and quality

In our consumption-crazed society, it's vital to teach our children how to be good consumers. By "good" I mean consumers who make wise, thoughtful buying decisions. Good consumers who understand the relationship between quality and price do research before making major purchases, and also have learned to overcome the urge to spend wildly and impulsively.

Like all life skills, savvy consumerism is a skill best acquired at an early age. That's why I urge parents to let their children spend the bigger bucks on more items such as expensive toys, clothes, stereos, and sports equipment. Why? Because I believe children need to learn from their mistakes. If they buy something on a whim and figure out later it was a waste of money, they may be more thoughtful next time. If they buy something of low quality, and it breaks down after a few weeks, they may learn to look for better quality. But if you always make the major buying decisions, they won't learn anything, and they will carry this lack of financial expertise into their adult years. So your first step is to let go a little. Let your children spend and learn. Make allowances for them!

A major purchase would be anything priced more than one month's total allowance. For example, if your child is getting $5 a week, a major purchase would be $20 or more. Any purchases below $20 can be made from the money in your child's wallet, while larger purchases should be made from your child's savings in the bank.

Slice of Life

During the month, perhaps you can keep part of the money in a safe place at home in case the child's wallet is lost or stolen. Patrick once lost his wallet while we were bowling. He would have lost $35 if his mother hadn't taken $20 to be put in his bank account. Lucky young man!

The Key Spending Principles

Spending Principle 1: **Plan ahead for major purchases.**

Spending Principle 2: **Do your homework.**

Spending Principle 3: **Consider price and quality.**

Spending Principle 4: **Give your child a month's leeway.**

Spending Principle 5: **Plan ahead for holidays.**

Spending Principle 6: **Teach tipping to reward good service.**

SPENDING PRINCIPLE 1

Plan Ahead for Major Purchases

Spending the bigger bucks on major purchases requires planning and forethought. If your child is interested in buying an expensive toy, for example, encourage her to take some time to think about it. Does she really want the toy? Is there something else she would like to buy instead? If she still wants the toy, perhaps there is a more appropriate model or brand available. Ideally, every major purchase should be planned over a period of weeks or even months. To help you teach this concept to your children, I've created The Wise Purchase Plotter (see Skillsheet 4.1). This form may help you and your children build a wish list of the things they want to buy, and to track what happens to the item after they purchase it. More on The Wise Purchase Plotter later in the chapter.

Slice of Life On a recent family vacation, each child saved $100 US to bring as spending money. The 13-year-old spent three quarters of the money; the 11-year-old spent all the money plus more; and the nine-year-old came home with half his money. Each child had a different way of managing money, but they all made their own choices.

SPENDING PRINCIPLE 2
Do Your Homework

Before your children spend the bigger bucks, they should do some homework. For example, if they want to buy inline skates, they should:

- visit a few different stores to find out the different makes and models
- go through consumer magazines and newspapers and clip out the advertising for inline skates
- talk to friends about what they have. Did their skates last long? Wear well?
- surf the Internet looking for different manufacturers and retailers
- compare prices. Find out how much each model/brand costs. Find out if there is a difference in prices from store to store. Find out why some types of skates cost a lot more than others
- find out if there are any sales on right now. When is the best time to buy inline skates? In the spring, or in the fall?

Help your children with this research, but let them do most of the leg-work. (This is great bonding time!) Even if they spend half an hour on the phone, it can be very productive. Encourage your child to speak directly to clerks and to ask questions. This process gives them confidence and helps develop their consumer skills as they get older.

Slice of Life   Older children can be taught to do the math to figure out and understand the cost of buying foreign currency, but our younger son complained about spending so much Canadian currency to purchase less foreign dollars. Buying at home can be smarter than buying in another country.

SPENDING PRINCIPLE 3

Consider Price and Quality

While your child is doing the research, explain the relationship between price and quality. In most cases, it's not wise to buy either the cheapest brand or the most expensive. The cheapest is probably of poor quality, and the most expensive brand is likely overpriced, even extravagant. Teach your children the importance of looking at both price and quality. Teach them to decide what level of quality they want, and how much they are willing to pay for it. They also have to understand, paradoxically, that the most costly is not always the best, and the cheapest is not always the worst.

Another buying decision we face relates to size. Talk to your children about reasons to buy the large box of cereal versus the smaller, more expensive one.

SPENDING PRINCIPLE 4

Give Your Child a Month's Leeway

As a parent, it's your job to help your child make major purchases, and to go through the decision-making process with them. However, for smaller purchases, you have to give your child some leeway. I recommend you let your child spend up to a month's allowance without interference. For instance, if your child gets $5 a week in allowance, allow him to accumulate up to $20 in his wallet, and to spend it as he chooses. If he has more than $20 in his wallet, the excess funds should be deposited in the bank. This one-month buffer will give your child the opportunity to learn from his experience, either good or bad.

SPENDING PRINCIPLE 5

Plan Ahead for Holidays

Trips and vacations can sometimes seriously undermine your allowance program. When you're on a one or two-week holiday, children will be constantly asking you to give them money, and the constant pestering can ruin your vacation. You'll find yourself saying "no, no, no." To avoid this scenario, help your children create a spending budget for the holiday. Have them save a specific amount of money (and perhaps promise to match it). Your children will put this money in their wallet, and use it to buy things on their holiday. This way, you don't have to decide what they buy and play the heavy every time you have to say "no." Let them make the decisions. And don't stand over them the whole holiday saying, "Don't waste your money on that!"

However, your children need to understand you won't be giving them any more money when theirs is spent. To help you with this process, I've created the kid's Vacation Planner skillsheet, which I will explain in further detail later in this chapter. Note: by matching their holiday savings, you create a powerful incentive for your children. They may save money by foregoing smaller purchases, or by earning more money around the house or neighbourhood. In addition, trips abroad are great opportunities to teach your kids about different currencies. If you are planning to visit another country, the holiday savings plan should include some discussion about the difference between the two currencies, and how that will affect the amount of money they will have to spend.

SPENDING PRINCIPLE 6

Teach Tipping to Reward Good Service

It's important for your children as consumers to understand the concept of tipping for good service. If they grasp the concept at a early age, they will learn to make a connection between value and financial reward. This will help them appreciate the hard work of others, and perhaps impress upon them the importance of providing value and service. When my wife and I go to a restaurant with our children, we discuss how tipping works, and decide together how much we should tip the server. If the service is good, we leave a tip of about 15 per cent, and if the service is poor, we leave a smaller tip. Most importantly, we discuss the tip together. In this way, our children understand how to show their appreciation of good service, and how to judge when the service is inferior. Next time you and your family are out for dinner, have your consumer-smart kids decide on the amount of the tip. (And let them figure out the math!)

The Wise Purchase Plotter Skillsheet

The best way to teach your children to be good consumers is to help them learn from their experience. Think about your own consumer choices. When looking back on purchases you made in the past, you may discover you bought the wrong brand, spent too much money, or purchased something you never use. This experience helps you to be more thoughtful about future purchases.

Skillsheet 4.1   *The Wise Purchase Plotter*

Item	Choices	Cost	Pros	Cons
	1			
	2			
	3			
	1			
	2			
	3			
	1			
	2			
	3			
	1			
	2			
	3			
	1			
	2			
	3			
	1			
	2			
	3			
	1			
	2			
	3			

To help your kids learn from their consumer choices, I've created The Wise Purchase Plotter found at Skillsheet 4.1. This form helps you and your children track a purchase from beginning to end. It is a helpful tool for teaching children to evaluate their need to purchase, the cost of the item, the differences in quality and the reason one item may be better than another. You may want to begin using the Plotter when your child says he wants to buy something, during the actual purchase, and three months later. After using the form a few times, your children will acquire a much better sense of what it means to be a good consumer.

The Kid's Vacation Planner

The Kid's Vacation Planner is designed to help your kids save and/or earn enough spending money for a holiday and can be found at the back of this book in The Skillsheets section. As I explained earlier, it's better for your kids to have their own spending money on a holiday. Starting a form when you begin planning the holiday months before will give your children plenty of time to get enough money together for the trip.

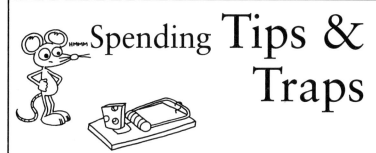

Spending Tips & Traps

1. Give your child the opportunity to make mistakes: Don't try to control the whole process. Don't make all of the buying decisions for your children.

2. Model good consumer behaviour: If you make spontaneous buying decisions, your kids will learn to do the same. If you want your kids to be good consumers, you'll have to be one yourself.

3. Go out for dinner and teach your children about tipping: Let your children assess the service and decide on the tip. Remember to let them know that when they are older, they might have a job waiting on tables. So they need to be good consumers and reward the servers for a job well done.

The Step-by-Step System

1 **Review your Allowance Contract**
- Review the list.
- Is it relevant?
- Add new items for consideration.

2 **Review and Plan for Upcoming Family Holidays**
- Plan your next holiday.
- Discuss holiday spending plan.
- Offer to match savings.
- Use the Kid's Vacation Planner.

3 **Talk about Spending Concepts**
- Plan ahead.
- Do your research.
- Discuss the relationship between price and quality.
- Discuss the one-month spending limit.

4   **Identify a Potential Purchase**
- Discuss the potential purchase.
- Explain how it will be paid for.
- Use the Wise Purchase Plotter.

5   **Research Potential Purchase**
- Help with information gathering.
- Visit stores to compare prices and quality.
- Read consumer reports.
- Help with making the best buy.

6   **Make Buy, Not-buy Decision**
- Decide with child whether or not to buy.
- Make purchase with child.
- Use The Wise Purchase Plotter.

7   **Assess Wisdom of the Purchase**
- After three months, use Plotter form again.
- Discuss the purchase with your child.
- Was it a good purchase?
- Why or why not?

CHAPTER 5

The Case of the Broken Window

3 MAJOR GOALS

Time to Implement: Two to three months

1 To teach your children to respect their own property, and the property of other people

2 To establish a consistent policy of consequences in the event your children violate a property rule

3 To teach your children appropriate behaviour in other people's homes, restaurants, hotels and other environments

It was bound to happen. Your child just smashed the neighbour's front window while playing ball. Your neighbour is really upset, your kid's upset, and now you're upset. In this situation, what do you do? Pay to have the window replaced out of your own funds, or have your child pay for it with his allowance? Was it an accident, or should you punish your child for being careless or deliberately destructive? There are no easy answers to these questions, which makes it even more important to establish rules with your kids about property rights. That way, when your child breaks a window, or shatters Aunt Nellie's china set, you'll know what to do, and your child will know what to expect. And hopefully, when your child reaches adulthood, he will have a healthy respect for his own property, and the property of others.

Now's the Time to Start

When your children reach five or six years of age, they start stretching their wings. They become more physically active, more curious and more experimental. They also become susceptible to the early stages of peer pressure. Under these circumstances, even the most angelic child will probably break something valuable. They will also lose things, find things, or even try their hand at stealing or vandalism.

At this stage, you have a choice. You can punish your child for every infraction, or develop a more subtle, graduated method of dealing with your child's early forays into the world of property rights. I suggest the second method, because I don't believe children should be punished simply for being children! I believe children should be allowed to make mistakes and learn from them. If children take responsibility for their actions, in some cases they should be rewarded, not disciplined. In fact, I think children should be punished only if they persist in their disregard for property rights. The key, of course, is to set the rules and teach them to your children.

The Rules of Property Rights

In my family, we have established guidelines regarding property rights. Over the years, we have used these rules to sort out all kinds of situations. For example, jumping or walking on the sofa means you sit on the floor. Stealing from a store means the child returns the item to the store owner. Breaking your brother's possession means you must help to pay to replace it.

Here's a summary of my suggested family policy with respect to property rights:

1. Everyone can make mistakes: even parents!
2. It's not a crime to make mistakes; it's only a crime not to learn from them.
3. Look after your stuff. Don't break it, bash it, or trash it.
4. Look after other people's stuff like it's your own.
5. If you break it, fix it. If you lose it, replace it.
6. Take responsibility for your mistakes. If you did it, admit it.
7. If you make the same mistake twice, you are going to help pay for it.
8. If you find something, turn it in.
9. Keep your bedroom neat and tidy. It doesn't have to be a jungle in there.

The Key Property Rights Principles

Rights Principle 1: **Make allowances for your kids.**

Rights Principle 2: **Use discretion and subtlety.**

Rights Principle 3: **Teach accountability and responsibility.**

Rights Principle 4: **Make your kids pay the second time around.**

Rights Principle 5: **Don't withhold allowance as punishment.**

Rights Principle 6: **Discuss the consequences with your child.**

Rights Principle 7: **Start with their bedroom.**

Rights Principle 8: **Teach the Golden Rule.**

Rights Principle 9: **Have your kids take a personal inventory.**

RIGHTS PRINCIPLE 1

Make Allowances for Your Kids

Don't punish your children just because they're kids. Remember, everyone makes mistakes. Allow your children some grace. Only punish/discipline them if they continue to exhibit the negative behaviour. For example, when our son was six years old, he took a comic book from a store without paying for it. He did a bad thing, but he didn't realise he had done anything wrong. Instead of punishing him, or berating him, I took him back to the store, had him apologise to the owner, and then I paid for the comic book. I also made my son understand the possibly grave consequences of stealing, and he got the message. He has never stolen anything again. If he had continued to steal, of course, I would have punished him. I would also have looked for contributing factors — had he been seeking attention more than usual or comparing himself to a new set of friends? This story illustrates the most important concept about kids and property. You have to "make allowances" for your children. Let them make mistakes — once or twice — without severe punishment, and only clamp down if they fail to learn from the lesson. Show acceptance, love, and help them understand what is the correct behaviour.

RIGHTS PRINCIPLE 2

Use Discretion and Subtlety

Base your response to a situation on the specific context of the moment. If your child accidentally breaks something, you probably shouldn't punish him. For example, if your child is telling an exciting story at the dinner table, and knocks his glass over onto the floor, and it breaks, it is obviously an accident. However, if he is throwing a football in the house and breaks a lamp, knowing that one of the house rules is 'no throwing balls in the house,' the child should be punished to some degree. The child can help repair or replace broken items. If it is the second time or a household rule has been broken, the child can pay for the cost of replacement. As I've said, if the behaviour persists, the level of punishment should be increased for each infraction. You have to use your discretion to decide what is appropriate in each circumstance.

| Slice of Life | Our kids painted their playhouse when they were 3 and 5 years old! They clean their soccer boots after a game. And once a week they give their bedrooms a thorough tidy-up. |

RIGHTS PRINCIPLE 3

Teach Accountability and Responsibility

Get your kids involved in caring for things they use regularly: show them how to:

- maintain their bikes
- wash the car
- paint the fence
- sew a button on a shirt

These are life skills that translate into care of property. The cost of maintenance is lower than the cost of replacement.

RIGHTS PRINCIPLE 4

Make Your Kids Pay the Second Time Around

In most cases, your child should only pay for something broken or lost if it is the second or third infraction of the same kind. In the first instance, the parent should pay for it. The second time, you can decide how much your child should contribute to the cost of replacing or fixing the property — based on age, the rules ignored and the circumstances. The amount will be based on the level of punishment you want to mete out, and on the ability of your child to pay.

Slice of Life

Over the last five years, each of our children has broken one of the glass panes on our front door. We have paid the repair bill, but they know the next time one is broken, the bill is paid by the one who broke it.

RIGHTS PRINCIPLE 5
Don't Withhold Allowance as Punishment

If you decide your children should pay for the damaged or lost item, don't take it out of their allowance. Require your children to earn the money by working around the house or neighbourhood. The experience of working off the debt will reinforce the lesson learned from the experience. Keep nagging down and savings up.

RIGHTS PRINCIPLE 6
Discuss the Consequences with Your Child

When your children break a property rule, ask them to decide what would be appropriate as a punishment. If they come up with it themselves, they will be more likely to learn from the experience as well. Of course, it will have to be close to what you would have decided. If your child comes up with too lax a punishment, then you can tell him what the "real" punishment needs to be.

RIGHTS PRINCIPLE 7
Start with Their Bedroom

I believe respect for property begins at home. If your children can develop respect for their own property, they will more likely show the same respect for others. So start by helping your child keep their room tidy. Kids or teenagers — they all need a little help! Don't let them leave their clothes and toys lying all over the room. Have them make their bed and do some basic cleaning. Provide them with shelves and drawers for their belongings. I think it's a cop-out for parents to let their kids go wild in their bedrooms. If your kids develop good habits in their own domain, it will translate into greater respect for property in all aspects of their lives. This not only makes them into good citizens, but great economic citizens because they will be a notch above their peers. Also, the cost of items for your home and your children should be reduced because they are being better cared for.

RIGHTS PRINCIPLE 8

Teach the Golden Rule

When your child shows disregard for someone else's personal property, teach them the Golden Rule. Ask him if he would like it if someone broke his toy, or stole his baseball cards. Help them to see the relationship between the feelings they have for their stuff, and how other people feel about their own things. This is especially useful when your child finds something and wants to keep it. Ask her: "If you lost something, would you want the finder to keep it, or return it to you?" If you ask her this question, she will probably realise quickly that she should try to find the rightful owner.

Slice of Life   A good time for your children to take an inventory of their possessions is after Christmas, birthdays, or during summer holidays when many new things are in their rooms. Also, it's a good time to think about giving things away or holding a garage sale. We held a garage sale once, and the kids all helped. We raised enough money to buy something we all wanted.

RIGHTS PRINCIPLE 9

Have your Kids Take a Personal Inventory

If your kids are like mine, they probably have a lot of stuff stashed all over the house. They probably own things they've forgotten about, or tend to neglect their property because they have so much. To instil a sense of ownership and pride in your child about their possessions, help them take a personal inventory. Have your child make a list of all of his major possessions. I find this exercise helps kids take greater pride in their possessions, and also helps them appreciate how lucky they are. You can use the Kid's Inventory Skillsheet found in The Skillsheets section at the back of this book or create a simple chart to complete this task.*

Reinforce Property Rights Before Special Events

Before going with your children to a restaurant, a hotel, or to visit a friend's house, hold a short meeting just before entering the new place. Ask your kids, "What is considered good behaviour when we are in a _____?" I find this short discussion in the moment translates into much better respect for property and results in a much more enjoyable visit for everyone. This is especially appropriate for children ages four to nine; after that, they probably know, and hopefully don't need a lecture.

---

*I have created a Kid's Inventory Skillsheet and it is available at www.makingallowances.com.

The Step-by-Step System

Teaching your kids about property rights will take months, perhaps years. However, if you consistently reinforce a specific policy in your family, your children will grow up with a well-developed respect for other people and their property. To assist you on this path, here are my suggested steps:

1 **Discuss the Concept of Property Rights with your Children**
Spend some time with your kids talking about:
- respect for their own property;
- respect for the property of other people;
- what will happen if they make a mistake and break or lose something;
- what will happen if they don't learn from their mistake and continue to break the rules;
- how and when they will help pay to replace or fix property;
- what they should do if they find something;
- other things which are not allowed such as stealing and vandalism.

2 **Set Rules for their Bedroom**
- Provide guidelines for a tidy room.
- Decide on the consequences of a messy room.

3 **Have your Children Complete the Kid's Inventory Skillsheet**
- Go through your children's belongings with them.

- List their major possessions.
- Teach them to care for these possessions.
- Help them set aside unwanted items for charity or a garage sale.

4 **Before a Special Event**
- Talk to them about appropriate behaviour.
- Ask them to describe the proper way to behave at a _____.

CHAPTER 6

The Gift of Giving

3 MAJOR GOALS

TIME TO IMPLEMENT: Two to three months

1 To teach your children how to give from their heart

2 To teach your children how to contribute to their community

3 To create a family system for giving to others on a regular basis.

Like all the good habits discussed in this book, the art of giving is a skill which is best learned at a tender age. To lead a meaningful life, all of us need to learn to give back something of ourselves to the world.

In my family, I've tried to teach my children the joy of contributing to their community, in both time and money. Each month, my boys give a portion of their allowance to the church and are involved in helping with community organisations. They also give away their unwanted clothes and toys to other children. These experiences have taught them how satisfying it is to do something worthwhile for others. They are learning how to give from their heart, not just out of a sense of duty or obligation.

And they are learning to look more outward to the world, not just inward to their own needs. Building relationships with people outside their own world will help them to see the bigger picture, and as adults they will be more empathetic. Teaching the gift of giving is an important way to instil a sense of balance in our children about money, material possessions and the greater experience of life and relationships.

Slice of Life

R.C.'s grandma sends a package of baking to her great-grandchildren every Christmas. When it arrives, it is always joyfully received by their hungry children. One year, the children sent their usual letter of thanks, but this time they went into their piggy banks and added some of their own money to the letter as a special gift to great-grandma. They were so excited to send this special thank you. Her reply came in the mail: "Thank you so much for thinking of me. May God bless you for your generosity. Remember, it is better to give than to receive. Love, Great-grandma." With the letter was a big, beautiful box of chocolates (this woman knows the language of children!).

The Key Giving Principles

To teach your kids the gift of giving, I recommend you start a system for regular donations, in both time and money. While the particulars will be unique to you and your family (such as what charities and community groups you choose), the system should observe these principles:

Giving Principle 1: **Give a set percentage of your income to charity.**

Giving Principle 2: **Give to charity on a regular basis.**

Giving Principle 3: **Give to a local charity.**

Giving Principle 4: **Get your kids involved physically.**

Giving Principle 5: **Help them to give the gifts.**

Giving Principle 6: **Help them choose an organisation with which they can relate.**

Giving Principle 7: **Give away unused clothes and toys.**

GIVING PRINCIPLE 1

Give a Set Percentage of your Income to Charity

When your children have learned to handle their allowance, by putting regular savings in the bank, they are ready to put aside a specific amount for charities. As a starting point, they could contribute five to ten per cent of their allowance to a charity every month. The actual amount could be higher or lower, as long as the percentage is consistent.

GIVING PRINCIPLE 2

Give to Charity on a Regular Basis

Your children will learn the gift of giving more effectively if they make their contributions on a regular

basis, perhaps once a month. I recommend the contribution be made to the same charity at least for the first
year or two. Examples of charities include: children's
charities, environmental groups, children's hospitals,
animal shelters and food banks.

GIVING PRINCIPLE 3
Give to a Local Charity

For your children to learn the gift of giving, they need
to see firsthand the positive results of their generosity.
That's why I recommend they give to a charity in your
community. If they can actually see the people they are
helping, and the positive results, they will experience
more profoundly the joy of giving. And this can then
be expanded to the world view.

GIVING PRINCIPLE 4
Get your Kids Involved Physically

While it's important for them to give financially, it's
also meaningful for your children to give of their time
as well. Find a community project or organisation that
needs volunteers and get your kids to sign up. If you
want, you can participate as well (your assistance may
be mandatory if your children are younger). This is
also a great opportunity for your kids to experience
giving as an independent activity.

GIVING PRINCIPLE 5
Help them to Give the Gifts

When it comes time to buy gifts for birthdays and special occasions, help your children buy their own gifts.

Don't do it for them. You can give them the money for the present, but they should buy it themselves. For example, let's say you want your son to give a birthday present to his sister or a friend. You can take him to the store and help him find something, or you can give him $10, $15, or $20 and tell him to find something on his own. Either way, your child will learn how to pick out gifts, and learn how it feels to give a present which took some time to find. In either case, you will provide the money, but your child will do the leg-work. Note: I don't think children should have to pay for gifts until they are about 12 years old. At 12 years of age, children are more able to earn extra money through babysitting, refereeing, doing yard work and delivering papers. With this new source of cashflow the child may want to buy gifts independently. Older children may decide they want to give on their own.

GIVING PRINCIPLE 6

Help them Choose an Organisation with which They can Relate

If your kids love dogs and cats, get them involved with the local animal shelter. If they love the outdoors, get them to join a local tree planting group. If they like learning, perhaps they can volunteer to teach other kids. The more interested they are in a particular area, the more likely they will enjoy giving their time.

GIVING PRINCIPLE 7

Give Away Unused Clothes and Toys

If your kids are like mine, they have a treasure trove of clothes and toys which they have outgrown or abandoned. It's a great exercise to have them sort through their stuff and pick out the things they don't need any-more. Take your kids to a local agency such as a women's shelter, children's hospital or local parent resource centre, and have them personally hand over the articles (you might want to phone first to determine what they are in need of). They will discover how sat-isfying it is to help other people in this way, and they'll be keeping their room cleaner at the same time.

Skillsheets and Exercises

Positive Blessings
The first step in learning the gift of giving is to appre-ciate how lucky you are. The more your children count their blessings, the more they will be inclined to give to the outside world. To help your kids take stock of their good luck, create a Positive Blessings* skillsheet where they can list the things for which they are grateful and then list the things that they will give. This exercise helps your kids literally count their blessings.

Gift of Giving Skillsheet
If you want your kids to give on a regular, consistent basis, they need to plan ahead. Help your children fill out The Gift of Giving skillsheet found at the back of this book in The Skillsheets section. Have them each

Slice of Life

One way to give is to plan a trip to the grocery store once a month. After your child pays for her treats, she can drop a coin (or coins) by the checkout; many char-ities have donation boxes there. You can also pur-chase food staples there and give them to the food bank.

*I have created a Positive Blessings Skillsheet and it is available at www.makingallowances.com.

decide on three ways they can help other people. For example, they can choose:

- a local organisation to give money to (and how much money to give)
- a community group to act as a volunteer
- an organisation to donate old clothes and toys

Giving Tips & Traps

1. Let your kids do it themselves: With your help, let them choose their charity and community projects. Let them do much of the work themselves.

2. Keep it in your community: Keep all of the projects as local as possible. The interaction with their local community will give them the best experience possible.

3. Help them be consistent: Use the forms to keep your kids on track. Regular giving is as important as regular savings.

4. Get them involved in something they like: You want them to enjoy the project for which they are volunteering. You want your kids to have a positive experience for their first time as a volunteer. It will give them the idea that giving can be fun and also helpful.

The Step-by-Step System

1

Decide on the Charity
- Help your child choose a charity.
- Make it local, if possible.
- Make it relate to a personal interest.

2

Determine Amount of Giving
- Help your child decide how much to donate each month.

3

Have your Child Choose and Volunteer for a Project
- Help your child volunteer for a local community project or organisation.
- Volunteer for a short- or long-term project.

4

Give Old Clothes and Toys to Charity
- Help your kids sort through their belongings.
- Go with them to take unwanted items to a local charity.
- Have them give their boxes of stuff to volunteers.

5

Make Financial Donation
- Have your older children start to make financial donations to their favourite charity.

6   **Complete a Positive Blessings Skillsheet**
- Have your kids write down things they're thankful for.
- Discuss how and why others are unfortunate.
- Discuss ways to help.

7   **Complete the Gift of Giving Skillsheet**
- List the three ways kids plan to help in the community.
- Use the form to identify regular donations and volunteering.

Slice
of Life

One family I know has a $5 limit for gifts for siblings at Christmas time. Hints are dropped, and snooping is done to find something meaningful for the other person. Parents give suggestions and help the younger ones make purchases.

CHAPTER 7

Credit When Due

---
3 MAJOR GOALS

TIME TO IMPLEMENT: Two to three months

1 To help your children understand how credit works

2 To help your children develop good borrowing and repayment habits

3 To give your children experience dealing with credit

When your children reach their late teens or early twenties, they will face their first major financial test as an adult. They will be deluged by a flood of offers to acquire credit in the form of credit cards, student loans and consumer financing.

How they deal with the sudden exposure to the world of credit could determine their financial success as an adult. If they've developed good credit habits, your children will pause before borrowing, and ask the key question: "Is this purchase worth the long-term obligation to repay the debt?"

On the other hand, if they have poor credit habits, or have no experience with credit, your adult children could fall into a credit trap. They could quickly rack up debts on multiple credit cards, over-extend their mortgage and spend beyond their means. Before you know it, your children could join the ranks of those people who are simply unable to manage credit. And believe me, their ranks are legion.

That's why this chapter on credit is included in this book. I believe children should learn about credit. They have to experience first-hand what it's like to borrow money for something, and then spend months paying back the debt. They have to learn that debt is a serious obligation. And they have to learn how it feels to pay off a debt for something which lost its appeal long ago. And if they can experience the world of credit in a small way, under your supervision, they will be more likely to deal more responsibly with larger credit issues when they reach their early adult years.

The Key Credit Principles

Once your children have acquired the skills and habits from the previous chapters, they will be ready to learn about credit. To teach your children about borrowing and debt, observe the following key principles:

Credit Principle 1: **Make it a positive experience.**

Credit Principle 2: **The loan should be repaid on time, and in full.**

Credit Principle 3: **Set a two-month credit limit.**

Credit Principle 4: **Establish a two-month term on the loan.**

Credit Principle 5: **Set out a clear repayment plan.**

Credit Principle 6: **Don't charge interest on family loans.**

Credit Principle 7: **No missed payments or defaults are allowed.**

Credit Principle 8: **Let them make mistakes.**

Credit Principle 9: **Only let them borrow from you.**

CREDIT PRINCIPLE 1

Make It a Positive Experience

Your child's first taste of credit should be a positive one. When the loan has been paid off (in full and on time), she should be proud that she has fulfilled her obligation. However, by positive, I don't mean the experience has to be painless. Your child may experience the pain of paying back a loan for something she shouldn't have purchased in the first place. In this sense, the experience will be positive because she will think twice about borrowing money again for something foolish.

And that's why it's so important your children have their first credit experience with you. You can control the size of the loan and the repayment terms. You can make sure your child only borrows an amount they can afford to repay. In this way, your child will be neither afraid nor incautious of credit in the future. They will begin to learn how to manage both the upsides and downsides of credit. Wanting to be free of debt but not scared of having debt is a great philosophy to live by.

CREDIT PRINCIPLE 2
The Loan Should be Repaid on Time, and In Full

One of the most important credit concepts your children need to learn is that a loan must be repaid. And it must be repaid within a specific time period. They need to learn that a loan is a serious obligation, that in the real world, loan payments must be made on time. So when you are collecting loans payments from your children, don't make any exceptions. Otherwise, they won't learn the key lesson about borrowing and debts: that a loan should not be entered into without some serious forethought.

CREDIT PRINCIPLE 3
Set a Two-month Credit Limit

As a rule, don't lend your child more than two months worth of allowance. For example, if your child gets $20 a month in allowance, set their credit limit at $40. You don't want them to overextend their short time frame. Note: older children may need a three-month limit.

CREDIT PRINCIPLE 4
Establish a Two-month Term on the Loan

The loan should be repaid within two months. If you make the term longer, your children may feel too great an impact from the payments. They may begin the nagging process again because they are short of cash for too long. Note: Older children may need a three-month limit.

Consider the temperament of your children. If you feel they won't be able to manage a short-term pay back, extend the time and adjust the payments. But remember that the point of this exercise is to teach your child the discipline (and experience the pain!) of paying back a loan. Stick to the program and when they nag, let them express their feelings. Be patient, and try not to get into debates or arguments. Emphasise that they have made an agreement and need to fulfil it.

CREDIT PRINCIPLE 5
Set Out a Clear Repayment Plan

To pay off the loan, your child should contribute half of her allowance, and earn the other half by doing odd jobs around the house. For example, on a $40 loan, $20 should be deducted directly from allowance, and the other $20 should be earned. (Note: if you don't have any odd jobs for your child to perform, set the credit limit at one month's allowance, and simply deduct half of their allowance over a two-month period.) However, it's best if your child has to do additional work because of the loan. This will allow your

Slice of Life

A number of my clients have used loans to their teenagers as a savings plan. When the teen repays their loan, the money goes into a savings plan for the teen. The teen never knows that the money is designated for them by their parents to help in their child's future. The parents continue to use that money for other loans, and finally give the money to the child when they feel it is appropriate.

child to experience paying for something after the initial excitement is gone and maybe foregoing something today!

CREDIT PRINCIPLE 6

Don't Charge Interest on Family Loans

Although you might want to teach your children about interest, this is not the time. I believe family loans to children shouldn't involve interest. At this stage, the goal is to teach your kids about borrowing and repayment, not about interest payments. Moreover, I don't think it's right for parents to earn interest from their children.

CREDIT PRINCIPLE 7

No Missed Payments or Defaults are Allowed

As I said previously, it's important that your child doesn't miss any payments or default on the loan. They have to learn that loans have to be repaid on time and in full. If you back down, they won't learn this lesson.

Slice of Life

Does your child have a great friend who just happens to come along on outings with your family, but often doesn't have any money? Our son does — and we like having this friend around because he's funny and respectful. To get around the no-money issue, we created some jobs for "Frank" to do, along with our son, to "pay-off" some of his "debts" to us. Frank never seems to mind doing the work, and we feel good that he is doing something constructive to acknowledge his appreciation for being included. Sometimes our son gets paid for the job done, and Frank doesn't, but both of them understand the arrangement.

CREDIT PRINCIPLE 8
Let Them Make Mistakes

When your child wants to borrow money to buy something which you consider foolish or misguided, don't meddle in her decision. Let her make the purchase, and live with the decision. This is part of the learning experience. If she regrets taking the loan, that's good. Your child will think twice about making the same mistake. If she is glad she took the loan, that's good too. She will be inclined to see credit as a way to get things she really wants. The key thing is: if you take a hands-off attitude, it is your child who will make the decision, not you. And that's how she will learn.

CREDIT PRINCIPLE 9
Only Let Them Borrow from You

Children should only be allowed to borrow money from their parents. They shouldn't borrow money from friends or from their brothers or sisters. If something goes wrong with the loan, they could lose a friend or get in trouble. To guarantee their first credit experiences are positive, make sure your children understand this important rule.

Of course, sometimes they will ask someone to lend them a dollar or two (a friend or a sibling) and you may not even know. But they should not be borrowing more than $5 from others.

Skillsheets and Exercises

The Kid's Loan Contract

This contract is similar to the Allowances Contract. Before giving out the loan, you and your child fill out this skillsheet and talk about what signing the form entails. A copy of the Kid's Loan Contract can be found at Skillsheet 7.1. You indicate the amount of the loan, the repayment terms and the schedule of payments. Both you and your child sign the contract. When the loan is paid off, the contract is returned to your child.

The Kid's Loan Repayment Planner

This skillsheet will help you keep track of the loan payments. As you can see at Skillsheet 7.2, the sheet indicates the payments deducted from allowance, and payments earned doing odd jobs.

Slice of Life

Our eldest son bought a CD player but needed a loan to get the one he wanted on sale. It happened that we were also going on a trip to see cousins in Philadelphia. He came to me and said that he could not pay back the loan because he had to save for the trip. I asked him if my banker would say that it was OK to miss my mortgage payments for the next couple of months while I went on a holiday. He grudgingly stuck to the loan agreement and he saved enough for the trip. Thus, he learned a positive lesson.

The Kid's Loan Contract

Skillsheet 7.1

(Parent) I, _____ will loan (child) _____ (amount) $ _____ to

purchase _____ .

THE TERMS OF THE REPAYMENT ARE AS FOLLOWS:

(Child) I, _____ will pay (amount) $ _____ per (week, month) _____

for (#) _____ (weeks, months) _____ , commencing (date) _____ .

_____ _____
Child   Parent

_____ _____
Date   Date

Note:
1. Chores _____
2. Work _____
3. _____

The Kid's Loan Repayment Planner

Skillsheet 7.2

AGREEMENT BETWEEN:

_____ (child) & _____ (parent)

TOTAL AMOUNT OF LOAN:

$_____

Date	Amount	Cumulative

REPAYMENT TO BE MADE IN FULL ON OR BEFORE

_____

The Step-by-Step System

1

Meet with your Children
Have a meeting with your children to discuss the concept of credit. Tell them you are willing to lend them two months of allowance to buy something bigger. Explain how a loan works and how it is repaid. Go over the other concepts discussed in this chapter. Note: your children do not need to have a purchase in mind in order to have this discussion. You are just explaining that you will be willing to lend them money if the need arises.

2

Prepare The Kid's Loan Contract
When your child approaches you for a loan, fill out the contract together. Determine the amount of the loan (two-months of allowance maximum), the amount and frequency of the payments and the date of the final payment.

3

Discuss the Reason for the Loan
Ask your child what the loan will be used to purchase. Don't judge the merit of the purchase, but discuss it with your child. Ask: "Why do you want this thing?" and "Do you think it is worth borrowing money?" Don't answer the questions for them, let them answer. Just engage them in the discussion. Be supportive even if you think the purchase isn't a good idea.

4

Lend the Money
Give your children the loan in cash, and have them sign the contract upon acceptance.

5   **Supervise the Purchase**
Go with your child to make the purchase.
Do this to ensure that the loan is used to
make the intended purchase, not for other
day-to-day spending.

6   **Collect the Payments**
When you are giving your child allowance,
deduct half of it as a loan payment. Enter the
payment in The Kid's Loan Repayment Planner.

7   **Assign Odd Jobs**
To cover the other half of the loan payments, assign extra jobs around the house,
and pay an hourly rate, or a set amount
per project. When the job is completed,
deduct the amount earned in The Kid's
Loan Repayment Planner. Note: these odd
jobs should be in addition to the regular
chores done by your child.

8   **Celebrate the Last Payment**
When your children make the last pay-
ment, celebrate it. Give them back the
Kid's Loan Contract marked "Loan Paid."
Have a little party. Offer congratulations.

9   **Discuss the Experience**
Talk to your children about the loan. Ask
them if they would borrow the money again
to buy the same thing. Do they think it was a
good idea or a bad idea to borrow the money?
What would they do differently in the future?
Do they want to take out another loan, or do
they want to save up their money first?

CHAPTER 8

The Debit Side of the Coin

3 MAJOR GOALS

1 To teach your children how to use a debit card properly

2 To teach your children how to maintain good savings habits even while using a debit card

3 To teach your children how to make well-considered consumer choices even when money is readily accessible

Although debit cards have spread like wildfire across our economy, I still think real dollars and cents are the best tools for teaching your kids about money. By handling dimes, quarters and paper bills, your children learn about money in a tangible way and in a much more comprehensive fashion. If your children use a debit card for most transactions, and rarely handle cash, there's a danger they won't learn important lessons about handling money. They could start using the bank machine like they use the refrigerator. When they're hungry to buy something, they will simply dip into the bank machine. They might eat up their savings by buying whatever strikes their fancy in the moment. All of the good habits you have been trying to teach them might get tossed aside once they get their hands on that little piece of plastic. And there's one more potential danger. If your child gets hooked on a debit card, it could lead to harder stuff: credit cards, store cards, frivolous consumer loans and other forms of floating credit. In other words, the debit card could set your child off in the wrong direction.

In spite of these debit card pitfalls, we as parents have to be realistic. We are moving toward a cashless future when most transactions will involve the transfer of electronic funds over computer networks. Almost every purchase — including houses, haircuts and hamburgers — will be made electronically. So instead of fleeing from this cashless onslaught, we also have to figure out how we can help our children grow up to be financially responsible adults in a cashless society.

And that's the great opportunity facing you as a parent. You can teach your children how to set their own limits on spending even if the funds are readily available with a simple swipe of a card. You can also teach them how to become comfortable with money as a virtual symbol rather than as a tangible commodity. Experts tell us that children begin to think more abstractly as they reach 10 years of age. Therefore, I encourage you to wait until your child reaches at least 10 (and some kids may need to wait longer) before providing them with a bank card. This will emphasise to them the responsibility and privilege that comes with this technology. Using the principles and approach in this chapter, you can teach your children how to use debit cards responsibly, a skill which will be extremely useful in their adult years.

The Key Debit Principles

Teaching your kids good money habits using debit cards instead of cash is a tricky business. All of the good things they've achieved could be thrown into jeopardy by that little card. So you have to proceed carefully. In my experience, I've found the following principles work well.

Debit Principle 1: **Teach your children responsible use of the debit card.**

Debit Principle 2: **Set limits on the use of the card.**

Debit Principle 3: **Use control mechanisms.**

Debit Principle 4: **Get the right kind of card.**

Debit Principle 5: **Don't use auto-deposit.**

Debit Principle 6: **Use short-term savings account only.**

Debit Principle 7: **Keep some cash in their wallet.**

Debit Principle 8: **Improve security with a debit card.**

DEBIT PRINCIPLE 1

Teach your Children Responsible Use of the Debit Card

Try not to introduce the debit card to your children until age 10 even if their friends have them (and your kids will want them!). You have to make sure they understand the rules of the road. Treat a debit card like a driver's license. Your children have to show they understand how to use a debit card properly before they get to use one. To start the process, begin by keeping the card for your children. Only let them use the card in your presence. That will give you the chance to discuss the dangers and opportunities presented by the card when they are using it. The most important concepts to teach them are:

- They should stick to their good money habits even if they have the card;

- They should still plan their purchases ahead of time. If they haven't set a goal for a major purchase, they shouldn't use the debit card to buy something on the spur of the moment;

- If they're not careful, the card might tempt them to buy a lot more than they can afford, which will eat up their savings;

- Bank machines are not refrigerators. They shouldn't go to the bank machine every time they want something;

- They should use the card to make deposits and withdrawals on a regular basis — an average of once a week, or even once a month.

DEBIT PRINCIPLE 2
Set Limits on the Use of the Card

Teach your children to set limits on how often they use the card, and how much they can withdraw at a time. I suggest you limit your children to one purchase or withdrawal per week, especially at the start. Make it clear: they shouldn't be running off to the bank machine every time they are out of cash.

DEBIT PRINCIPLE 3
Use Control Mechanisms

Fortunately, it's possible to set limits on the debit card when you get it from the bank. You can set the card to:

- only accept deposits, not withdrawals or purchases;
- limit the daily amount of withdrawals (to only $20 a day for example);
- limit the amount of a point-of-sale purchase (such as $100 a day).

These limits can be changed as your children begin to demonstrate responsible use of the cards.

DEBIT PRINCIPLE 4
Get the Right Kind of Card

Different financial institutions offer different kinds of debit cards. They are not all the same. I suggest you find a debit card which offers:

- no transaction fees (there are some institutions which will waive the fees on debit cards and savings accounts for children);
- insurance on items purchased with the card which will cover loss, theft or breakage for a limited time following the purchase;
- an extended warranty on purchases which enhance the manufacturer's warranty.

If you can't find a debit card with all of these features, try to get one with at least one or two of them.

<hr>

DEBIT PRINCIPLE 5

Don't Use Auto-deposit

Although many adults have their salaries deposited directly into their bank account by their employer, don't have your children's allowance transferred from your account to their accounts. Keep giving them cash. Have them maintain the same routine which you started in Chapter 1 with The Allowance Contract. You still want them to make their own deposits so they can learn from this activity.

When your children are in their teens, you can start the process of auto-deposit. Good money habits should be in place by then. Younger children need the tangible use of money to comprehend the value of money. This was the discussion I had with one of our friends who wanted to have the bank automatically deposit money into their children's account each month. Even though this will save you time and hassles, resist this virtual transaction for your younger children (and some teens). It will jeopardise their learning good money habits needed for the future.

DEBIT PRINCIPLE 6

Use Short-term Savings Account Only

Only have one account (the short-term savings account) accessible by the debit card. You don't want your children using the debit card to withdraw money from their medium- or long-term savings. That's a recipe for financial meltdown. Have the bank put medium-term savings into rolling 30 day term deposits to safeguard the money. Have your children put their long-term savings into mutual funds.

DEBIT PRINCIPLE 7

Keep Some Cash in their Wallet

Your children should still keep some cash in their wallets or purses. I suggest a maximum of $20. This is still enough for a week's activities and not too much to lose! This amount may vary from family to family, but what is important is to set a limit.

DEBIT PRINCIPLE 8

Improve Security with a Debit Card

Better safety and security is one major benefit of a debit card over cash. A debit card can protect your children much better than cash against loss and theft. To improve this level of safety I suggest you:

- limit the amount of daily withdrawals and purchases;
- teach your children to keep the existence of the card and their PIN number to themselves;
- teach your children to avoid flashing their money in public places;
- teach your children to be careful at the ATM machine

Keep an Eye on the Future

If there is one thing we've learned about technology, it's always changing. Just when we get used to bank machines and debit cards, a new way to spend money electronically rears its head. Within a few years, we will see the emergence of smart cards which store funds in a computer chip on the card. You will be able to use these cards for parking meters, vending machines and just about anything else you can imagine. As well, you will be able to download the funds into your card from your bank account over the Internet or through a card reader on your telephone. When that day comes, we will be one step closer to the cashless society. And hopefully, the lessons you teach your children about debit cards will help them be good money managers even when dollars give way to bits and bytes.

Staying on the Debit Side of the Coin

Using a debit card wisely is one of the most important skills your children need to learn about money in our modern society. It will prevent a financial and emotional drain on you today and in the future. If you take the time now to teach your children how to use a debit card properly, your children will be much better equipped to prosper in the twenty-first century when dollars and cents may be just the whimsical interest of historians and antique collectors.

The Step-by-Step System

1   **Discuss the Pros and Cons of Debit Cards with your Children**
Explain how debit cards work, and the rules for using them. As I've suggested, begin by allowing your children to use the card only in your presence.

2   **Go to the Bank**
When your child is ready to sign up for the debit card, accompany him or her to the bank.

3   **Choose the Right Debit Card**
If possible, find a debit card which has no transaction fees, and offers insurance and warranty protection on purchases.

4   **Choose the Limits on the Card**
Ask the bank to set limits on the amount which can be withdrawn or used for purchases on any given day. Limit access on the card to your child's short-term savings account.

5   **Have your Child Keep Some Cash**
Encourage your child to keep a maximum amount of cash on hand. I've suggested $20 earlier, but each family will need to decide what is right in their circumstances.

6   **Limit Card Use to Once a Week**
You can give the card to them once a week, and have them return to it to you after they've used it. When they are older and also more responsible, you need not hold their card for them.

7   **Review Goals and Priorities with your Child**
Reinforce the importance of sticking to the long-term plan even though money is more easily accessible using the debit card.

CHAPTER 9

Building the Money Mountain

----
3 MAJOR GOALS

TIME TO IMPLEMENT: *Two to three months*

1 To teach your children how to make better choices about spending money

2 To help your children learn the basics of budgeting

3 To teach your children the importance of long-term savings

My definition of financial maturity is simple: it's the ability to give up instant gratification in order to realise long-term dreams and goals. It's the maturity to recognise that big goals do not happen on their own, they require small sacrifices everyday. We now want our children to expand their money management skills to incorporate long-term savings.

As a parent, I think it's vitally important to give your children this ability, especially in the realm of money. They must learn how to create a simple budget, and how to divide their money into short-, medium- and long-term funds. In so doing, they will hone their decision-making skills. They will learn how to decide how much money to spend today, how much to save for a large purchase or a holiday, and how much to invest in long-term savings such as a mutual fund.

If you and your children have been following the concepts in this book, they will be ready to take this step.

The Key Money Mountain Principles

Money Mountain Principle 1: **Teach your children budgeting basics.**

Money Mountain Principle 2: **Help your children set financial goals.**

Money Mountain Principle 3: **Teach your children the fine art of choosing.**

Money Mountain Principle 4: **Divide money into distinct categories.**

Money Mountain Principle 5: **Discuss the concept of the money mountain.**

Money Mountain Principle 6: **Get professional advice.**

MONEY MOUNTAIN PRINCIPLE 1

Teach your Children Budgeting Basics

Budgeting and cash flow management are big words, especially when you are 10 or 11 years old. But they are actually very simple concepts. A budget helps you decide how you will spend the money you receive on a regular basis (weekly, monthly, annually). Cash flow management helps you put your money in the right places so you will have enough for everything you want to do. Both of these concepts are important for your children to learn at an early age — a process aided by the use of the Kid's Cash Flow Skillsheet at the back of this book in The Skillsheets section. It will take them many years to learn how to budget and manage their cash, but if they start at a young age, they will be well-equipped to manage their money properly when they reach their late teens and early twenties.

MONEY MOUNTAIN PRINCIPLE 2

Help your Children Set Financial Goals

Having a goal makes all the difference in managing money. If you have a long-term goal in mind, you are more motivated to make day-to-day sacrifices in order to achieve it. Without a goal, you may spend money frivolously, and never save anything for a rainy day. As such, you have to teach your kids how to set goals for their money. In other words, it's not so important what the goals are, it's the act of setting goals that's important.

MONEY MOUNTAIN PRINCIPLE 3

Teach your Children the Fine Art of Choosing

Because the things we want to buy are infinite, and money is usually finite, making choices is the only answer. And how well we make choices can greatly affect our future. That's why it's so important to teach your children good decision-making skills: how to list options, how to compare them, how to make a decision and how to live by that decision.

Of course, decision-making skills are important in all areas of life, but they're especially important in the world of money. At this stage, your children should learn they have to think about where they want to put their money. Do they want to spend it all today or save it for a new skateboard? Do they want to save it for a holiday next month, or put it into a mutual fund? If they can develop their decision-making skills early on, they will make better decisions as adults.

MONEY MOUNTAIN PRINCIPLE 4

Divide Money into Distinct Categories

Teach your kids to divide up their money into three areas:

1. Short-term money for things such as candies, comic books, movies, snacks and other small purchases. Approximately five to ten per cent of this category should be allotted to charity.
2. Medium-term money for larger purchases such as CDs, holidays, toys, sports equipment, clothes and other major purchases.
3. Long-term money to invest in mutual funds or other investments, as well as for larger purchases such as a car, university or taking a dream holiday.

At this point, your kids should understand the difference between short- and medium-term money. Their short-term money can be held in their wallets, while the medium-term money is saved in their bank account until they need it. This money is saved from their allowance and from doing odd jobs, as discussed in Chapter 1.

When creating their budget, you can work with them to decide how much money to put into each category. For example, you could divide the money as follows:

1. Short-term Money — 50%
2. Medium-term Money — 25%
3. Long-term Money — 25%

While it is probably quite easy for your kids to save their money in the bank for large expenses like holidays or sports equipment, it's quite another matter for them to save their money for the long-term. At 10 years old, the idea of saving money just for the sake of it can sound almost ludicrous. "What's the point in putting your money in the bank if you never take it out?" he may ask. At this point, you have to explain the value of building a money mountain.

Some children will want to spend 100 per cent on short-term gratification. That is why they need to have goals and dreams to save for. Each family and each child may determine different percentages but the emphasis will remain the same. Also, if your child is saving for a specific item or event she may put up to 75 per cent toward it. Talk with your child so that she can learn from experience.

MONEY MOUNTAIN PRINCIPLE 5

Discuss the Concept of the Money Mountain

The benefits of long-term savings (from the perspective of a 10-year-old) are:

- You will earn money on your money (interest);
- Your mountain will start getting bigger and bigger, faster and faster (compound interest);
- You will own part of many different companies (mutual fund/share ownership);
- You will be able to use these funds for really important things like going to college, buying a car or going on a great trip.

When your kids are making decisions about money (what to buy and when), it's important that they view the process as a positive one. Instead of looking at money as something they just spend as it comes along, budgeting will allow them to look ahead and decide beforehand how they want to divide up the money that will be coming. The habit of looking ahead, instead of from day-to-day, is an extremely important money management skill, which should be learned early in life.

Slice of Life   Early in 1998, we had a family discussion about the Olympics to be held in Australia in 2000. Jan and I have talked about going to Australia since we were first married, and the kids were excited about seeing the Olympics live because they dream of one day participating in track and field or soccer at an Olympic level. We agreed that getting to the Olympics was a goal we all wanted to work toward, so we started to put medium- and long-term savings away for that special trek.

MONEY MOUNTAIN PRINCIPLE 6

Get Professional Advice

When your child is ready to begin putting money into long-term investments, I suggest you seek out a professional advisor. If you have your own financial advisor, he or she will probably be the ideal person to work with. Go with your child to meet with the advisor, and get him or her to explain the basics of investments. This will give your child some experience dealing with professional advisors, and will establish in her mind how investments are different from putting money in the bank.

The Step-by-Step System

1

Explain How a Budget Works
Talk with your child about why you need to create a budget using the Kid's Cash Flow skillsheet in The Skillsheets as a start. Stress that a budget will allow your child to have enough money for the things they want, while saving money for the future.

2

Establish a Goal or Goals
Help your child set some financial goals over the medium-term and long-term. List some things he or she would like to save for over the next six months to a year (holidays, new bike, sports equipment), and what they would like to save for over a period of years (college, a car, an extended trip).

3

Explain How to Divide Money into Three Categories

Help your child understand the three categories of money (short-term, medium-term and long-term).

4

Decide on How Much to Allocate to Each Category

Help your child to determine the distribution across the categories. I suggest:
- 50% for short-term needs;
- 25% for medium-term needs;
- 25% for long-term savings.

5

Create a Budget*

Help your child to create a budget for allocation of funds over the next six months. Enter the amounts which will be allocated each week in the three categories. Add up the savings in the medium- and long-term categories. Indicate the expenditures planned for the medium-term category. Add up the money which will be invested in long-term savings over the six month period.

6

Meet with Your Financial Advisor

Go with your child to visit your financial advisor. Have your advisor explain how mutual funds work, and how they are different from savings accounts. Open a mutual fund account in your child's name.

---

*I have created a Kid's Budget Planner and it is available at www.makingallowances.com.

7   **Create an Investment Tracker***
Create a ledger in which to record your child's investments in mutual funds. Each time they receive a statement, they can record the value of the fund. In this way, they can see how the value of their investments goes up and down depending on conditions in the market.

8   **Review Past Budget and Make New Budget**
At the end of six months, sit down with your child and review the success of the previous budget. Discuss how to do the budget differently. Fill out a new budget for the next six months.

---

*I have created the Money Mountain Builder and it is available at www.makingallowances.com.

CHAPTER 10

The Investment Crystal Ball

---

3 MAJOR GOALS

TIME TO IMPLEMENT: Two to three months

1 To teach your children the habit of long-term savings

2 To teach your children basic principles about investing in mutual funds

3 To establish an investment account for your children

In Chapter 9, Building The Money Mountain, I introduced you and your child to the concepts of budgeting and long-term savings. If your child has started putting money away for the long-term, it's time to teach him about how to invest the money to get a better return than with a low-interest bank account. Although there are many investment options available, I recommend you start by teaching your child about mutual funds. Mutual funds are popular because professional fund managers work to realise higher rates of return for your investment. For children, mutual funds are also the best introduction to an investment vehicle because they are relatively easy to understand, and there is plenty of information available in newspapers, magazines, books and on the Web. As time goes by, your child's mutual fund account will facilitate a lot of learning for the whole family. Children tend to ask a lot of questions.

The example of a pizza is helpful in understanding mutual funds. Imagine several of us give money to the pizza maker for a slice of pizza each. Together we can buy a whole pizza, and the pizza maker manages the making and baking of the pizza. Mutual funds are similar in that many investors pool their money (like the pizza buyers), and invest, and then the fund manager (like the pizza maker), looks after the fund (the pizza).

The purpose of this chapter is to help you explain mutual funds to your kids, and also to give you some advice on how to proceed with making an actual investment for your child.

Although I provide basic principles for choosing mutual funds, I do not make any specific recommendations about actual funds or mutual fund companies. Consult your financial advisor for the best course of action, taking into account current market conditions and your individual risk preference.

The Key Investment Principles

To teach your kids about long-term investing in mutual funds, follow these principles.

Investment Principle 1: **Set an exciting goal for the money.**

Investment Principle 2: **Put away 25 per cent of available money.**

Investment Principle 3: **Stress the no-withdrawal rule.**

Investment Principle 4: **Don't put the money into an RESP.**

Investment Principle 5: **Don't put the money into an RRSP.**

Investment Principle 6: **Make lump sum contributions.**

Investment Principle 7: **Use a financial advisor.**

Investment Principle 8: **Choose mutual funds run by experienced managers.**

Investment Principle 9: **Choose international/global funds.**

Investment Principle 10: **Explain the basic concepts of mutual funds.**

Investment Principle 11: **Use the Internet to research funds.**

Investment Principle 12: **Get the grandparents involved.**

INVESTMENT PRINCIPLE 1

Set an Exciting Goal for the Money

To motivate your children to put money away for
many years to come, your children must have an exciting goal in mind. Remember, they aren't saving money
for retirement. They are saving for something which
will happen when they are about 18 to 25 years of
age. For example, the money could be used for:

- a car;
- a trip to Europe;
- their university education;
- a down payment on a house;
- starting a business.

You may come up with another goal, but the key is to
decide on something definite. Ultimately, your children might use the money for something else, but the
goal will keep them motivated.

I also recommend you write out this goal, and even
name the investment account something which relates
to the goal such as The New Car Fund, or The
European Vacation Program. That will keep everyone
focused on why your child is investing the money.

INVESTMENT PRINCIPLE 2

Put Away 25 Per Cent of the Available Money

When you are investing money for the long-term,
there is a fine line between investing too much and
investing too little. If you invest too much, you will
eventually want to scale back, which can erode your
confidence. If you invest too little, you won't be able
to reach your goal soon enough. Either way, you will
be disappointed. As a rule, financial experts advise

adults to put away 10 per cent of their income into long-term savings. This may seem enough for your children at this stage. However, I believe that if children are able to save 25 per cent when they are young, saving 10 per cent as an adult will seem easy. Figure out how much money your child will have available from allowance, gifts and jobs, and determine 25 per cent of that amount. Use the Kid's Investment Calculator found at the back of this book in The Skillsheets section or keep your own records of the source and amount of your child's accumulated savings. The Kid's Investment Calculator shows the principal amount saved by the child, as opposed to the mutual fund statement sent out by the company, which shows both principal and interest. Having both clarifies how hard your money is working.

INVESTMENT PRINCIPLE 3
Stress the No-withdrawal Rule

One of the key rules in long-term investing is the no-withdrawal rule. That means the investor should not withdraw the funds from the long-term investment account until he is ready to use it to achieve the desired goal. It should not be withdrawn when the whim arises for vacations or consumer purchases. Your child should understand that if the money goes into the investment account, it doesn't come out until the goal has been reached. This is a critical principle which must be explained to your child right from the start.

Slice of Life

One grandparent we know transferred $100 worth of his mutual funds to each of his grandchildren as a Christmas gift. He also gave each of them another gift — providing them with one long-term gift, and one short-term.

INVESTMENT PRINCIPLE 4

Don't Put the Money into an RESP

Although I endorse the use of an RESP (Registered Education Savings Plan), and discuss it fully in Chapter 12, I do not recommend such a plan for this exercise. For the most part, money put into an RESP comes from the parent (or a grandparent) directly, not out of the money held by the child. The purpose of investing in mutual funds is to help your child learn about investing, and to develop investing habits which will carry over profitably into their adult years.

INVESTMENT PRINCIPLE 5

Don't Put the Money into an RRSP

There is no advantage for your children to put money into an RRSP until their income is higher than $30,000 a year, or they are over 18 years of age. In an RRSP, the money is sheltering taxes while the child is in the lowest tax bracket, and may be taken out later when your child is in a higher tax bracket, resulting in higher tax costs. While the child is under 18 years of age, the money has to be held in trust by an adult.

INVESTMENT PRINCIPLE 6

Make Lump Sum Contributions

Although it is advisable for adults to make regular monthly payments to their RRSP and mutual funds, regular contributions are not applicable to this situation. Instead, when your child has accumulated a size-able amount (over $100) in their long-term savings account, make a lump sum investment in a mutual fund. In this way, your child makes a conscious decision to invest the money. This action reinforces the reasons for making the investment, and gives your child ongoing experience making investment decisions. Hopefully, when your children are in their twenties, the systematic habit is established.

INVESTMENT PRINCIPLE 7
Use a Financial Advisor

Although it's now possible to buy mutual funds directly over the Internet and by telephone, I recommend that you seek out the assistance of a qualified financial advisor. The advisor will help you choose the appropriate funds, and help explain to your child how mutual funds work. As well, your child will learn how to interact with a professional financial advisor, a skill which will be invaluable in the future. For that reason, I suggest you and your child visit your advisor in person.

INVESTMENT PRINCIPLE 8
Choose Mutual Funds Run by Experienced Managers

Make sure you choose mutual funds which are run by managers with at least 10 years of experience. You are more likely to realise a higher rate of return with an experienced manager. So instead of looking at the short term rates of return, find out who is manager of the fund. Has he or she been with the fund for many years? Is he or she the one who was running the fund when it achieved the previously high rates of return? If the manager used to run another fund, find out the performance of the fund under their administration.

INVESTMENT PRINCIPLE 9
Choose International/Global Funds

When you are choosing the investment, look for funds which invest in companies around the world. A global fund will likely achieve higher rates of return because they can move money from one market to another around the world as conditions change. Ask your advisor to show you the long term returns and the risk associated with each fund.

INVESTMENT PRINCIPLE 10
Explain the Basic Concepts of Mutual Funds

Before you make an investment, it's important to explain mutual funds to your child in terms she can easily understand. I have learned that children understand the following concepts about mutual funds:

- An investment in a mutual fund usually earns you more money over the long term, than leaving the money in the bank.
- The reason you invest in a mutual fund is because the value of your investment will probably go up over the long-term.
- Money invested in mutual funds is used to purchase stocks of companies on the stock exchanges that are doing business around the world.
- If the companies are profitable, the value of the mutual fund goes up as the underlying stocks go up.
- Each mutual fund invests in a bunch of different companies. For example, if the fund is like a pizza, each company in the fund is like one slice of the pizza.

- The person who runs the mutual fund — the fund manager — decides which companies to add to the fund.
- You want to find a fund manager who knows what it takes to make a company succeed (what ingredients are needed).
- If your fund manager can successfully choose companies over the long term, you will earn more money on your investment.

Don't be too concerned if your child doesn't grasp these concepts completely at first. These lessons will become clearer with experience. Every time your child makes a lump sum investment, or receives a statement, they will learn more about how mutual funds, stock markets and economic cycles work.

INVESTMENT PRINCIPLE 11
Use the Internet to Research Funds

Although I recommend you use a qualified financial advisor, I do advise you to spend some time with your child on the Web looking at different mutual funds. This experience will teach your child how many funds are available, and show him how to compare different funds.

INVESTMENT PRINCIPLE 12
Get the Grandparents Involved

I think it is very important for grandparents to help teach your kids about money, and especially about long-term investing. When your children hear from a grandparent about the importance of investing for the long term, they have a living, breathing reminder that they have a long future ahead of them. If possible, the grandparents might be interested in contributing part of the money to be invested in the child's mutual funds account.

The Step-by-Step System

1　**Meet with your Child**
Talk to your child about putting part of their long-term savings into a mutual fund account. They will need $100 initially, and $50 lump sums thereafter. Explain how mutual funds work.

2　**Set a Goal for the Investment**
Help your child envision a big goal for the investment such as a car, a trip overseas, a down payment on a house, or a university education.

3　**Decide How Much to Invest**
Determine the amount of money to be put into mutual funds. I recommend at least 25 per cent of the child's total amount of money available from allowance, gifts and jobs.

4　**Search the Internet for Mutual Funds**
Surf the Net with your child, looking at different mutual funds. Use this exercise to show your child all the different mutual funds available.

5   **Visit your Financial Advisor with your Child**
Go with your child to speak with your advisor. Have your advisor explain mutual funds to your child.

6   **Choose the Mutual Funds**
Together with your child, select from the funds recommended by your advisor. Choose funds which are global in nature, and run by experienced fund managers who have managed the fund for more than 10 years.

7   **Set up the Mutual Fund Account with your Advisor**
Assist with putting the first lump sum payment into the account.

8   **Make an Initial Contribution to the Account**
You can get a mutual fund account started for as little as $100.

9   **Make Lump Sum Contributions to the Account**
When your child has accumulated a sizeable amount in his long-term savings account, make another lump sum contribution to the investment account. Don't worry about making regular contributions. Just make contributions when your child has sufficient funds. If you want to be consistent, consider making a lump sum contribution every three months. These contributions will depend upon your child's source of income.

10 **Review Account Statements with your Child**
When you receive a statement from your advisor, or from the mutual fund company, go over the document with your child. Discuss the reasons why the account went up or down.

11 **Review the Investments Annually**
Every year, perhaps around your child's birthday, review the mutual funds in your child's portfolio. Decide together if you want to keep the same funds, or add the money to other funds. If you decide to add, talk to your advisor along with your child.

If you observe these principles, and follow this step-by-step system, your child will learn about mutual funds, develop the habit of investing for the long-term, and achieve an important first investment goal. As well, it's likely you will learn more about investments and mutual funds yourself.

CHAPTER 11

Taking Stock

3 MAJOR GOALS

1 To teach your children about how the stock market works

2 To teach your children how to choose the right stocks

3 To help your children understand the difference between speculating and long-term investing

Up to this point, I've advised you and your kids to stick with mutual funds for your long-term investments since it's best to have professional fund managers choose the stocks for you. However, your kids might be interested in choosing their own stocks and in learning more about the stock market.

If your kids want to get into the stock market and make their own trades, you need to teach them some basic principles. Otherwise, your kids might see the stock market as some sort of gambling casino where they move in and out of the market on a daily basis (i.e. commodity trading, penny stocks and e-trading). They may want to buy speculative stocks, thinking to ride them up and make huge profits. However, they are more likely to ride them down again, losing what they might have made. All of this trading will quickly deplete their savings. Your kids could also buy into the wrong stocks at the wrong time. And they may never learn how to properly research and choose the right companies. They may join the ranks of investors who are addicted to the excitement of the market, but rarely make any long-term gains in wealth.

On the other hand, if your kids want to put money into the stock market, you have a great opportunity to teach them how to do it right. You can help them develop their own process of researching and selecting good blue-chip stocks based on the opinions of experts. You can help them see the difference between speculation and long-term investing. And you can help them develop an in-depth understanding of how the stock market operates — knowledge which could be extremely useful in their careers. If you have been burned, or have stayed away from the stock market, here is a way of developing a strategy with your child which is right for you.

The Key Stock Market Principles

Based on my experience as a financial advisor, I've identified a number of key principles which will help you teach your kids about the stock market.

Stock Market Principle 1: **Help your kids with their homework.**

Stock Market Principle 2: **Articulate your investment ideology.**

Stock Market Principle 3: **Discourage gambling.**

Stock Market Principle 4: **Focus on blue chip stocks.**

Stock Market Principle 5: **Create a dummy portfolio.**

Stock Market Principle 6: **Develop a step-by-step method and rating system.**

Stock Market Principle 7: **Enlist a professional advisor.**

Stock Market Principle 8: **Go for the long term.**

STOCK MARKET PRINCIPLE 1

Help your Kids with their Homework

No, I'm not talking about school homework. I'm talking about doing research on companies before you buy their stock. If your kids want to invest in a particular company, help them search for information on the Internet, at the library and with a brokerage house. Get the company's annual report. Help your kids find out the history of the company, how the stock has been performing, the prospects for its industry and how the company markets its products and services. Get the opinion of investment experts. If possible, visit the corporate headquarters of the company.

Attend trade shows. With some of this research, you and your kids can decide if this stock still looks like a winner.

STOCK MARKET PRINCIPLE 2
Articulate your Investment Ideology

Doing research on companies is a great way to learn about the world, and how it operates. If your kids are going to pick their own stocks, it's important for them to invest in companies they believe in. Ask your kids if they want to put their money into companies that make and sell tobacco, liquor, weapons or chemicals. Do they want to invest in companies that pollute the environment or clear cut forests? Do they want to support companies which exploit children in the underde-veloped-world? If not, perhaps they're interested in supporting companies with progressive labour practices, or firms which make environmental products. Articulating their values will help your kids choose stocks which make them feel good, not just make them rich.

Slice of Life

My eldest was looking at the annual report from one of his mutual funds and was surprised to see that Microsoft was not on the fund's list of companies. I explained that the professional money manager choos-es companies that they believe will rise in price and incur less risk during industry and market corrections. Obviously, the manager felt that there were other com-panies they would choose first. Since then we have watched which high tech stocks fund managers are choosing.

STOCK MARKET PRINCIPLE 3
Discourage Gambling

Many people use the stock market as a casino. They jump in and out of the market ten times a day. They're not investors, they're speculators. You don't want your kids to turn into investor-junkies so you need to point out the dangers of speculating. Explain how hard it is to pick a winner from a bunch of high-risk stocks. Compare speculating to gambling. Remember to point out that you only hear about the one winner, while the thousands of losers don't speak up.

STOCK MARKET PRINCIPLE 4
Focus on Blue Chip Stocks

When you are researching stocks with your kids, make a clear distinction between blue chip companies and all the rest. Explain how blue chip companies are household names with excellent prospects for long-term dividends and growth. Point out how blue-chip stocks tend to rise steadily in value while speculative stocks rise and fall like a wild roller coaster. Stress how well-run blue chip companies bounce back quicker from an economic down-turn. Teach your kids that it's better to invest for the long term in a well-established company.

One way to make this point clearer is to have your kids name the companies they've heard of before — companies which make the products and services they buy. Have them do some investment research on these companies. Find out how they've performed on the stock market during the past ten years or more.

STOCK MARKET PRINCIPLE 5
Create a Dummy Portfolio

Before your kids put money into the stock market, have them try it as a game first. Set up a dummy portfolio with 10 or less stocks. Pretend to buy the stocks and keep track of how they perform. When your kids buy and sell, factor in the brokerage fees and taxes to see their real net gain. Keep tabs on the total value of the portfolio over time. If you want, you can create a portfolio for each child, including different stocks in each one. Chart the different performances of the portfolios. When your kids are confident they understand how to invest in the stock market — based on the positive performance of their phantom stocks — then they can use their real money. If possible, set up these portfolios on a computer using a spreadsheet program or use a program from the Internet.

STOCK MARKET PRINCIPLE 6
Develop a Step-by-Step Method and Rating System

The best way for your kids to build their portfolio is by helping them to design their own methodology for selecting stocks. Work with your kids to write out ten steps they will use to help them select a company (based on their own interests and concerns — for example they may want to pick only environmentally sound companies, or they may think high tech companies are best). Create a checklist and a rating system. This will help them in making choices about stock selection and also in assessing reasons to sell the stock.

STOCK MARKET PRINCIPLE 7
Enlist a Professional Advisor

Even in this day of discount brokers and e-trading, your kids should learn to heed the advice of seasoned brokers and investment counsellors. When your kids have selected some potential stocks, have them speak to an advisor. Get good advice. Does this stock really have potential? Is there something about this company they've missed? Get the facts and a second opinion before they invest any money.

STOCK MARKET PRINCIPLE 8
Go for the Long Term

Investing for the long haul is the most important lesson you can teach your kids about the stock market. Encourage your kids to pick companies with a solid future. Encourage them to ride the economic ups and downs of the market each year, knowing that the companies they have chosen have been around for a long time and have solid potential.

The Step-by-Step System

1 1. Discuss the difference between speculating and long-term investing.

2 Discuss the difference between speculative stocks and blue chip stocks.

3 Set up a dummy portfolio.

4 Identify potential company(s) for investing.

5 Conduct research on each company using the Internet, newspapers, annual reports and by talking with financial advisors.

6 Track performance of companies in the dummy portfolio (create a blue chip and a high-risk portfolio).

7 After one month or two, assess the results of the dummy portfolio.

8 Choose companies for real stock purchases.

9 Do additional research on these companies.

10 Buy shares in the company(s) sharing the greatest potential.

11 Track the price of the stocks on a weekly or monthly basis.

12 Assess the performance of the portfolio on an annual basis.

CHAPTER 12

A Future So Bright

Hmmmmmm......

This way to the future

3 MAJOR GOALS

Time to Implement: *One to two months*

1 To begin saving for your children's post-secondary education

2 To decide on the best type of educational savings plan

3 To express to your children the importance of higher education

In the twenty-first Century, a post-secondary education will be very important to ensure your child's bright future. But the cost of tuition and other education-related expenses is rising exponentially every year as governments cut back on subsidies. According to statistics, in 1998, 60 per cent of students graduated with an average debt load of $25,000, making Canadian students the most indebted in the western world (Association of Universities and Colleges of Canada, 1998). When your child reaches university age, it may cost $25,000 or more for each year of university or trade school. Planning ahead is essential. You have to start saving when your child is still in primary school or earlier. The question is: "What is the best way to save for your child's education?" There are generally two methods: through a Registered Education Savings Plan (RESP) or through an In Trust For (ITF) account.

Although this chapter is not directly related to teaching your child about money, an education fund is an essential tool to help fund your child's success in the future. As well, the very existence of the fund will act as a powerful message to your child on the importance of education and your hope for their success.

The RESP Explained

A Registered Education Savings Plan (RESP) is a program supported by the Canadian federal government. The purpose of the program is to help parents save

Slice of Life

Over ten years ago, Jan and I started an RESP for our children. It was a small amount at first, but it has grown steadily over the years. Our boys know about the account and we discuss it when the statements come. This has created an internal motivation to pursue higher education without our preaching about it.

money to fund their child's university or college education. You can set up an RESP through your financial advisor or at most banks. Parents contribute to the plan on a regular basis (usually monthly). The beneficiaries of the plan can be any child in your immediate or extended family. More than one child can be included in the plan. As well, the beneficiaries can be changed at any time.

The money in the plan can be invested in mutual funds or other investments. Any interest or capital gains earned within the RESP is sheltered from tax. (But unlike an RRSP, you do not receive a tax deduction for money contributed to the plan.) In addition, the principal can be withdrawn at any time in case of an emergency. The plan can benefit from the grant the government is providing for each child. They will contribute 20 per cent on top of your RESP contribution, to a maximum of $400 per child. They pay this directly to your plan.

That's the good part. On the flipside, an RESP has several restrictions and stipulations which you should consider carefully before proceeding. The maximum amount of money which can be contributed to an RESP is $42,000 per child. You can contribute for 21 years, but your plan matures in 25 years. Having a single plan versus a multi-person plan has some risks if your one child chooses not to further his education. In the 1999 federal budget, changes allowed for greater flexibility if the fund is not used toward your child's education. Discuss this fully with your financial consultant.

Most importantly, the money earned in the RESP, the non-taxable interest, should be used for expenditures such as tuition, books and computers. The principal which you invested in the fund can be used for other expenses such as room and board, travel costs and a monthly allowance!

The ITF Explained

An ITF (In Trust Fund) is an informal trust plan for your child. Money contributed to the plan can be invested in mutual funds, treasury bills and almost any savings investment vehicle. You can contribute as much as you wish to this plan. All capital gains accrued within the plan are considered (for tax purposes) as income earned by your child, not by you. And because a child doesn't usually have a significant income, little or no tax is paid. Interest and dividends earned by the plan are attributed back to the contributor (you) for tax purposes. In this plan you need to invest in capital gain growth investments. See your financial advisor for more information on this option.

This kind of trust is an excellent alternative if you have only one child, or if you simply don't like all of the restrictions placed on an RESP. For example, if your child does not attend university, you will not forfeit any money from the plan. Your child can use the money for something else. However, an ITF is missing two major benefits of the RESP: the 20 per cent matching contribution from the government and access to the ITF once the child reaches the age of majority.

If you are looking at these two types of savings plans — an RESP or an ITF — I recommend the following: if you have one child, go with the ITF; if you have more than one child, go with the RESP. With multiple children, it's much more likely that at least one of your children will go to university or a trade school. If you have only one child, anything is possible, and you may risk forfeiting the tax-free interest you earned within the plan. (Note: provided certain conditions are met and do not change, you can transfer the money in the plan to your RRSP.)

The Key Education Savings Principles

When you decide to set up an education savings plan, base your decision on the following principles:

Education Savings Principle 1: **An education savings plan sends your child an important message**

Education Savings Principle 2: **Get grandparents and other relatives involved**

Education Savings Principle 3: **Don't ask your child to contribute**

Education Savings Principle 4: **Make regular contributions**

Education Savings Principle 5: **Keep it confidential**

Education Savings Principle 6: **Stress the value of saving for the future**

Education Savings Principle 7: **Consult your financial advisor**

EDUCATION SAVINGS PRINCIPLE 1

An Education Savings Plan Sends your Child an Important Message

When you set up an RESP or an ITF, it stresses the importance of education to your child. It serves as a gentle nudge in the right direction, and can help motivate your child to become a dedicated student. An education fund is a strong symbol of your hope in your child's future: a message which will not be lost on your child.

EDUCATION SAVINGS PRINCIPLE 2
Get Grandparents and Other Relatives Involved

If grandparents sponsor or contribute to the fund, your child will feel the whole family is behind her education. Ask them if they want to get involved. (Trimark Mutual Funds revealed in a recent survey that 65 per cent would likely contribute to a grandchild's education.)

EDUCATION SAVINGS PRINCIPLE 3
Don't Ask your Child to Contribute

Your child should not be asked to contribute to his own education fund. Like allowance, an RESP or ITF is something which is given to the child for simply being part of the family. This is part of building a family legacy, and provides a step up for our children.

EDUCATION SAVINGS PRINCIPLE 4
Make Regular Contributions

Regular contributions (monthly or quarterly) to an education fund will result in higher returns over the long-term. By making consistent contributions, you will take advantage of a concept called Dollar Cost Averaging, which effectively averages out the ups and downs of the investment market. (We parents, of course, are to do this with our RRSP contributions.)

EDUCATION SAVINGS PRINCIPLE 5
Keep It Confidential

Teach your child not to tell friends about the details of the RESP. Your child can tell other people she has a plan, but not about the amount of money in it. Your child needs to learn early to maintain a certain level of privacy and discretion when it comes to personal finances.

EDUCATION SAVINGS PRINCIPLE 6
Stress the Value of Saving for the Future

An RESP or an ITF is another great way to teach your kids about the importance of saving money for the long term and to see how it grows over time. If possible, get a graph from your financial advisor which shows how tax-free interest can make a savings plan grow exponentially.

EDUCATION SAVINGS PRINCIPLE 7
Consult your Financial Advisor

Don't set up an education fund without the help of your financial advisor. He or she will help you decide on the best option (RESP or ITF), the right amount to contribute (based on your income) and what investment vehicles to use (mutual funds, T-bills, stocks).

Slice of Life

I will never forget one panic stricken call from clients about their child's costs for university, and their concern about how to pay for it. I went to their file and discovered that they had been contributing to an RESP for over ten years. We had forgotten about the plan we set up so long ago. Both of their children graduated with their education paid for.

A Long-Term Plan for Higher Education

Although most parents these days understand they play a key role in the education of their children (it can no longer be delegated solely to teachers), many parents still don't realise they will also have to take more responsibility for the financial costs of higher education. Rightly or wrongly, governments are no longer willing or able to carry the load, so a lion's share of the responsibility lands with parents. As I've emphasised in this chapter, the best strategy is to start early, and contribute regularly to an education fund. When the time comes, you will be glad you had a long-term plan for your child's education.

The Step-by-Step System

1 Discuss the Education Fund with your Children

Tell your children you want to start saving money for their college education. Explain in simple terms how the plan works. If you started a plan when your children were infants, begin to discuss it with them when they are school age.

2 Visit your Financial Advisor

You may wish to take your teenager along with you.

3 Choose an RESP or ITF

Along with your advisor, decide which type of plan is best for your situation.

4 Choose Start Date, Trustee or Beneficiaries

Decide on the details of the plan with your advisor.

5 **Make your Investment Decisions**
Invest the funds in mutual funds with a global reach. Work with your advisor to determine the appropriate investments.

6 **Get Relatives Involved**
See if grandparents or other close relatives want to contribute to the plan.

7 **Start Slowly with Contributions**
Begin by contributing an amount which you can part with every month. Like all long-term savings programs, it's always easier to increase the amount than to scale back.

8 **Show Statements to your Children**
When you receive a statement for the plan, show it to your children. Plot how the total has been increasing over time.

CHAPTER 13

The Kid's Business Builder

---

3 MAJOR GOALS

TIME TO IMPLEMENT: Two to six months

1 To develop your children's entrepreneurial spirit

2 To teach your children basic concepts about business

3 To give your children first-hand experience running a simple business

When your children grow up, it's a good bet they might become business owners. As we progress through the twenty-first century, I believe the level of employment in the corporate and public sector will continue to shrink, while the small business sector will continue to expand. Read any business newspaper or magazine for articles on this subject. When your children graduate from high school or university, they may face a tough job market. But that doesn't mean they will suffer from a lack of opportunity. Instead of looking for a job, they may simply start their own business and make their own opportunities.

If your children are going to prosper in the entrepreneurial future, they need to learn at an early age how to discover a need in the marketplace, how to develop a product or service to meet that need, and how to get the word out that they are open for business.

To build confidence and independence, your children will also need to develop the right attitude: an entrepreneurial attitude. They need to learn how to act on their ideas. They have to learn success in life is only really possible if they are prepared to provide value before expecting anything in return.

I believe you should expose your children to entrepreneurial ideas at an early age. With your guidance, you can help your children experiment with small business ventures so they will learn from their successes and from their failures. If you help your children start thinking like entrepreneurs at a young age, their future will be bright indeed.

Slice of Life   Justin, a 16-year-old neighbour, has had a business called "Lawncutter will Travel" for many years. He mows the lawns of neighbours within a four-block radius, and brings his own mower with him.

The Key Kid's Business Builder Principles

Business Principle 1: **Make learning about business fun.**

Business Principle 2: **Turn your kid's odd jobs into a business.**

Business Principle 3: **Help your kids set up their business.**

Business Principle 4: **Work closely with your child on the business.**

Business Principle 5: **Don't create jobs in competition with adults.**

Business Principle 6: **Talk with your child about the business regularly.**

BUSINESS PRINCIPLE 1

Make Learning about Business Fun

If you want your kids to learn, fun is the number one ingredient. The same goes with business. I'm always astounded how so many people make business so dreary, serious and money-focused. I think running a business should be fun. And if you want your kids to take an interest, you definitely have to make it an enjoyable experience.

Playing board games is a great way to teach your kids about business. I suggest you start with Monopoly. In my opinion, it's the best business-oriented game ever invented. Your kids will learn how to buy and sell property, how to pay and charge rent (watch out for Park Place!) and how to handle the ups and downs which come with every roll of the dice. I also recommend other games such as Risk, StockTicker, Yahtzee, Careers, Payday and The Game of Life.

All of these games introduce kids to the world of business without being too technical or serious. Your kids will learn important skills such as decision-making and relationship-building, and yes there may be a little yelling and screaming. They'll also learn how to come up with new ideas, and take action on those ideas.

When you're playing these games, draw your children's attention to the following concepts:

- Business is about providing value for other people;
- The price of a product or service is set by what people are willing to pay;
- Business doesn't always work out as expected: sometimes people won't buy your product or service and adjustments may be needed;
- Sometimes you have to lower your price, or negotiate (haggle) with the customer;
- You can be successful at business if you work hard.

BUSINESS PRINCIPLE 2

Turn your Kid's Odd Jobs into a Business

If your children are 10 to 12 years of age, they are probably already earning money from odd jobs such as lawn cutting or babysitting. I suggest you help them change these "jobs" into a "business." If your daughter is earning money from raking leaves, help her set

---

Slice of Life   One summer we held a garage sale. Each of the kids put items in to sell and helped to price them. The day of the sale, we made a float for change, set out the sale items, and the children took turns being cashier. It was fun, and we made over $100, which was used to buy something on which they had jointly agreed.

up a "leaf-raking" business. If your son is babysitting, help him set up a "child-care" business. The work won't change, but your child will view it as a business instead of a job.

If you are stuck for a kid's business idea, try reading *Fast Cash for Kids* or *Moneymakers*. (See the Other Resources at the back of this book for more information.) These excellent books contain a wealth of ideas for a kid's business.

BUSINESS PRINCIPLE 3

Help your Kids Set Up their Business

When you help your children set up their business, keep it simple. We're not talking about a multinational conglomerate here. Just a simple little business like a lemonade stand, or a dog-walking service. To set up the business, you and your child need to do the following:

1. Give the company a name: i.e. The Lemonade Company, or Doggie-On-A-Leash.
2. Write down a short description of the product or service such as "We walk dogs around the neighbourhood for you while you're busy, and give them a brushing so that they look good."
3. Set a price for the product or service. Have your child write down three reasons why the product or service is good value for the price.
4. Make up a flyer and/or a business card using this information.
5. Distribute the flyer in the neighbourhood.

The Kid's Business Builder skillsheet, located in The Skillsheets section, was designed to help you and your children set up their first enterprise. It will walk you through the steps. The Kid's Business Builder is basically a simplified business plan format which will help your child build a venture.

BUSINESS PRINCIPLE 4
Work Closely with your Child on the Business

Your involvement in your child's first business venture is extremely important. Get involved in every aspect of the process. Help her come up with the name, the description and the price. Help her make up the flyer and distribute it. At this stage, you want to make sure that your child feels totally supported. Remember to let her drive the process and the ideas.

BUSINESS PRINCIPLE 5
Don't Create Jobs in Competition with Adults

When you and your child decide what business to start, make sure it doesn't compete with something done by companies run by adults. So avoid full lawn care, dog grooming, comprehensive house cleaning, or other more advanced services. Stick to a simpler and smaller service like raking leaves, car washing, snow shovelling or weeding. It's important to avoid direct competition with adults because you want your child's first experience in business to be a positive one, not a competitive one.

Slice of Life

Herb's grandsons contacted their neighbours to arrange a weekend to have their homes and patios power-washed. Then they rented the power washer with borrowed money and worked over the weekend. After paying back the loan, each of them earned over $100 for the service they provided.

BUSINESS PRINCIPLE 6

Talk with your Child About the Business Regularly

Check in regularly with your child to see how his business is doing. Ask him what he is learning, and answer any questions he has. The more interest you show in his business, the more he will realise the importance and fun of running a business. As well, if you show enthusiasm, he will be naturally more enthusiastic.

Business Tips & Traps

A few circumstances may affect your child's business venture, so be prepared to address them.

1. Not Ready: If your child says he doesn't want to start a little business, let it pass for the time being. Concentrate instead on playing fun-filled business-oriented games. Also encourage him to continue doing odd jobs in the neighbourhood. At some future date, your child may be more prepared to see such activities as a business.

Slice of Life   Have a cake after dinner to celebrate, or present the child with a special gift to acknowledge her accomplishment. Make sure you give her lots of praise!

2. Homework: At this stage in life, school work is more important than making money. Your child should not neglect her school work in order to run her own business or do odd jobs. Encourage your child to spend time on her business after she has done her homework.

3. Holidays: Like adults, kids need time off too. So don't forego holidays or other free time to accommodate your child's business venture. You need to teach your children that rest and relaxation is just as important as hard work and effort.

4. Safety First: Before you let your child take on any business activity, consider carefully the safety issues. Is your child old enough to handle equipment such as a lawn mower? Is it safe for him to be on out on the street washing cars? Should she be wearing gloves if she is cleaning up a garage? Teach your child right from the start that safety is an important consideration in every job.

5. Business Loans: Your child may need a small sum of money to get his business started. He may need money to buy supplies such as lemonade mix, or equipment such as a leash for dog walking. If this is the case, give your child an interest-free loan to be paid back when he starts making money.

Helping our children to be creative, proactive and hardworking will enable them to reach higher goals for themselves, and to discover their unique talents and interests.

The experience of running a small business will give children concepts and understanding to learn to create value in everything they do. They may even create a vision or dream for their working future. In the short term, it provides them with real experience to enhance their résumé. So encourage your children to create their own business. The rewards will be great!

The Step-by-Step System

1 Plan a Family Night
As a family, set a date for a night to play business-oriented games. Talk about the different games and decide which one you want to play.

2 Go Shopping for a Game with your Children
If you don't own the game you decided upon, go with your children to buy it. Garage sales and thrift shops are good places to look for used games. Libraries sometimes lend games as well.

3 Play the Game as a Family
When you are playing a game such as Monopoly, talk about the business concepts they are learning. Ask them what they like and don't like about business. On other occasions, play other games such as Risk, StockTicker, Yahtzee, Careers, Payday and The Game of Life.

4 **Ask your Child if He Would like to Start a Business**

After you have played several business games, ask your child if he would like to run his own kid's business.

5 **Review and Choose a Business Idea**

With your child, write down all of the possible business ideas such as raking leaves, walking dogs, a lemonade stand, odd jobs, babysitting, or car washing. Remember, don't choose a business which will compete with adults. You want to keep it as simple as possible. Look at books for additional ideas. (Other Resources at the back of this book offers some suggestions for books.)

6 **Set a Goal for the Business**

Goal-setting is one of the most important things in a business. Help your child decide her goals for her business such as to:

- have fun;
- earn enough money to buy a new bike;
- sell $20 worth of lemonade;
- get business from five of your neighbours.

7 **Name the Business**

Come up with a name for the business which clearly explains what the business does, such as The Car Wash Kid, or The Rake People. Write the name of the business at the top of The Kid's Business Builder skillsheet located at the back of this book in The Skillsheets section.

8 **Write a Description of the Product or Service**
Help your child write a few sentences about what the company does. "I will shovel your driveway every time it snows this winter. I will also put down salt and clear off your steps too!"

9 **Set the Price**
Decide how much you want to charge for the product or service. Talk with your child about what would make a good price. If it seems too high or too low, discuss it with your child and arrive at a more appropriate price. You may decide to let them try it their way first and later change the price if necessary. Remember their first experience needs to be positive and successful.

10 **Write Down Why the Product or Service is Good Value for the Price**
Have your child write down three reasons why the price is justified. For example, $5 is a good price for raking your leaves because:
• there are a lot of trees in your backyard;
• your backyard is really big;
• will need to spend one hour or more to do a good job.

11 **Make a Simple Flyer**
Using pencils, pens, crayons or a computer, help your child make up a simple flyer for their business. Let them write down the information and put pictures on it. Try to avoid doing it all yourself, but offering some assistance is fine.

12   **Help your Child Distribute the Flyers in your Neighbourhood**
Walk around with your child and hand out the flyers to your neighbours. Help your child explain what the business is all about. Don't distribute the flyers too far from where you live. Stay close to home. (Safety is important!)

13   **Keep an Eye on your Child's Progress**
Closely monitor your child's business. Make sure you are comfortable with the people he is dealing with. Get to know the neighbours your child is doing work for. Do everything you can to make sure your child feels supported. However, don't do the actual work for your child.

14   **Ask your Child Questions about Her Business**
After your child has been doing her business for a while, ask her lots of questions about it. Do you like running your own business? What do you like about it? What don't you like about it? Do you think the price is right? Do you think you don't get more business because you charged too much? Do you think you could add more value? How could you provide your product or service to more people? What other business ideas do you have?

15   **Celebrate the Success of the Business**
At an appropriate time, celebrate the success of the business with your child. Reward and acknowledge your child for their entrepreneurial spirit.

CHAPTER 14

The Family Compact

3 MAJOR GOALS

TIME TO IMPLEMENT: Two to six months

1 To develop a family method for making important decisions

2 To build up your children's confidence and self-image through participation in family decision-making

3 To teach your children how to be team players

Learning to work together with others is perhaps one of the most important skills we all have to learn. We have to learn how to work through our differences of opinions, not only with our friends and business associates, but also with the people we love the most: our family. I believe co-operative decision-making is something parents must teach their children, and most often, these decisions involve money.

In the traditional family of the past, it was usually the father who made most of the financial decisions in the family. It has only been in recent decades that the mother has had a say in these matters. Well, now I think it's time we let our kids into the process as well. I strongly believe children need to be involved in some critical decisions in order to boost their confidence and self-image. If you, as a parent, can demonstrate to your children that their opinion counts, they will begin to take greater ownership and responsibility for the decisions which are made.

Let me be clear on this matter. I'm not saying children should be part of every financial decision made in the family. In fact, this can be severely damaging, especially if the family is going through a period of financial stress. There's no value in putting pressure on your small children. They won't know how to decode this information, and may feel your money problems are somehow their fault.

What I am saying is this: bring your children into the inner circle of the family to help with some of the financial decisions. For example, let them be involved in discussions about family vacations, big consumer purchases and other large ticket items. Have them participate in deciding between a new television set or a week at a resort. Or between buying a new or used car. Rate the pros and cons of ideas together. You'll be amazed how your children will respond. Your final decision as a parent may not be exactly what your kids want, but there is great value in obtaining their contribution. Children of all ages can give input, but you may choose to give older teens more weight in the decision-making process. In my family, I've noticed my children have learned important decision-making skills, and they are much more accepting of the decisions because they understand why they were made.

I call this type of co-operative decision-making The Family Compact. All of the principles discussed in this chapter about The Family Compact are meant to strengthen your family relationships, and to reinforce your shared values and interests. In other words, you are making a "compact" to work together as a family, not just as a group of individuals living together under the same roof. This can help when your children are teenagers, because that's when they definitely have their own opinions. If you bond as a family, you will build a secure place for the children to express themselves and be heard by their parents. You'll be helping to create a little harmony in life.

Slice of Life	We were in search of a Toyota van and had five dealerships looking over five weeks with no results. My middle son and I were on our way to a soccer practice when he spotted a Toyota van at a Honda dealership. We spoke to a salesperson and signed the deal in ten minutes, subject to Mom's approval. I told my son that because of all my research I knew the price we should pay. He did an inspection of the van and found four things damaged so we put them in the contract to be fixed as part of the deal. Mom gave her approval, and my son and I secured a great deal for the family.

The Key Family Compact Principles

The Family Compact is meant to help you and your children work together to make important financial decisions. But it is also about more than just money. The Family Compact is about co-operation, sharing, togetherness and collective values. Here are the key principles of a family compact:

Family Principle 1: **Children should participate in important family decisions.**

Family Principle 2: **Let your children dream of BIG futures.**

Family Principle 3: **Promote realistic expectations.**

Family Principle 4: **Working together will reinforce shared values and togetherness.**

Family Principle 5: **Proactive is better than reactive.**

Family Principle 6: **Create themes to establish context and to promote enhanced learning.**

FAMILY PRINCIPLE 1

Children Should Participate in Important Family Decisions

As I said in the introduction, children will develop confidence and a better self-image if they are included in the process of making important financial decisions. They will learn how to judge the pros and cons of a potential purchase. They will learn how to choose among a number of different purchases, and to understand it's not always possible to get everything you want. They will also come to appreciate that everyone has differences of opinion — even within a family — and that it's important to learn how to negotiate these issues without fighting or bitter feelings.

FAMILY PRINCIPLE 2
Let your Children Dream of BIG Futures

I believe it's important for children to learn how to think big. They need to be encouraged to dream of doing or achieving something really ambitious and exciting. For example, in my family, we have been dreaming of visiting Australia for the last 15 years. This has been one of our big, long-term goals, and within the next few years, we are going to make it to the Land Down Under. From this experience, my boys are learning patience, and the lesson that big goals are achievable, but they may take more time to achieve. So when you are creating a wish list with your children, let them dream big dreams. It will give them the confidence that almost anything is possible if they are willing to put in enough time and effort.

FAMILY PRINCIPLE 3
Promote Realistic Expectations

While it's important to let your children dream big dreams, it's also a good idea to promote expectations which are realistic for your family situation. Obviously, if you are on a tight budget, you shouldn't lead your children to believe they will be going on a round-the-world trip any time soon. If they are disappointed too often, your children will no longer be willing to participate in the process. They won't believe in it, and you want to avoid cynicism in your children at all costs. So it's your job to manage their expectations. Help them see, based on your budget, what is possible in the short- and medium-term. The trick, of course, is to honestly communicate your family's circumstances, while not stifling your children's big, more long-term dreams.

FAMILY PRINCIPLE 4

Working Together will Reinforce Shared Values and Togetherness

If you work together to make important financial decisions, you and your family will learn a lot about each other: what's important to each person; what things and activities they value; and what dreams and aspirations they have. Collectively, these discussions will help craft and strengthen your family's collective value system. It will also teach your children that it's fun and worthwhile to work together as a family, and this can only help them in building lasting family relationships when they become adults.

FAMILY PRINCIPLE 5

Proactive is Better than Reactive

When it comes to money, being proactive is an excellent habit. Instead of making big buying decisions in a few days or hours, it's better to plan them out over months and years. If you plan ahead, you will be able to schedule them better, and take advantage of seasonal sales and bargains.

FAMILY PRINCIPLE 6

Create Themes to Establish Context and to Promote Enhanced Learning

In our family, we create themes for each year in order to better channel our interests and activities. Each year, we meet as a family to brainstorm ideas for a theme. One year, we decided to make archaeology the theme. We read books on the subject, visited a dinosaur museum, participated in an archaeology expedition and did all kinds of other activities related to this subject. My kids learned a tremendous amount about archaeology and had a great time (we did too!). It also made it much easier for us to come up with ideas for activities and it gave a stronger context to our collective decision making.

In addition to its obvious educational value, the theme idea has many other benefits. I find it allows us to do a lot of activities which involve little or no money. We spend a lot less time in shopping malls and theme parks, and it has cut down on television time. We also have more fun together as a family, and create life-long memories.

Skillsheets and Exercises

The Wish List*

When you get together with your children to start your family compact, create a Wish List skillsheet to help everyone put their dreams on the table. Together, have everyone write down what they want to buy or do in the next 10 years. Make it a fun exercise. Don't judge the merits or drawbacks of any idea. Let every-

Slice of Life

On a trip to Hawaii, our children wanted to go surfing at $50 an hour. We asked them, "Do you want to do that or use the money to go on a snorkelling trip?" We discussed the pros and cons, and everyone then decided to go snorkelling.

*I have created a Wish List Skillsheet and it is available at www.makingal-lowances.com.

one dream big dreams. You can do this exercise annually. It's fun and helpful to compare ideas and values
as they change each year.

The Critical Decision Maker
Once you and your family have exhausted all of your
ideas on the wish list, rate the pros and cons of each
idea, prioritise them, and schedule them. The Critical
Decision Maker skillsheet, found in The Skillsheets
section at the back of this book, can aid in this task.
This exercise helps you decide what actions are necessary to achieve your key decisions, such as making
specific purchases, holiday plans, celebrations and
household improvements.

The Family Theme*
Create a Family Theme skillsheet to help you develop
themes for your family each year. Having a central
focus each year can be a fun way to learn and grow
close as a family. This skillsheet involves listing theme
ideas and some related activities. For example, you
could have a year devoted to:

- trees
- transportation
- history
- geology
- music
- geography
- pets or other animals
- farming
- architecture/heritage

*I have created a Family Theme Skillsheet and it is available at
www.makingallowances.com.

- the seaside (oceans)
- the rainforest (Canada has one too!)
- hiking
- outdoor sports
- space
- a specific country or place you plan to visit
- the Olympics
- fashion

Family Compact Tips & Traps

1. Plan regular events: When you create a family theme, plan regular events related to it. Creating a family compact is not just about making decisions about money, it's about being together as a family. You will want to plan one-on-one activities as well, where you can spend some individual time with your kids: a walk, a drive, or a trip to the pizza place.

2. Emphasise the importance of the long-term: When you are making your family compact, it's an excellent opportunity to teach your children about long-term planning. That's why it's important for you to help them dream big dreams. If they can believe anything is possible over the long haul, they will be more patient and confident.

The Step-by-Step System

1 **Get Together for a Meeting**
- schedule a meeting at a convenient time for everyone
- bring paper and pencils
- ask everyone to bring the Wish List
- bring the Critical Decision Maker skill-sheet

2 **Explain the Concept of The Family Compact**
- discuss the family compact idea
- explain how you will work together to make decisions
- show appreciation for your family's input
- model negotiation by allowing everyone to offer suggestions and work toward compromise

3 **Fill Out a Wish List Skillsheet Together**
- take turns contributing ideas to the wish list
- don't judge or criticise any ideas
- just brainstorm!

Slice of Life

One family we know began setting aside $50 per month to enable their teenager to go on a costly high school band trip. It took two years to save the money, but the teen was able to go, and to appreciate that a long-term goal requires patience!

4 Choose the Most Important 20 Wishes and Put them on the Critical Decision Maker Skillsheet
- from your wish list, go around in the circle and have each person choose the most important wishes from the list
- give each person their choice in turn until you have about 20 wishes
- ask everyone to collectively rate the wishes from 1 to 10
- come up with an average score for each wish

5 Discuss, Prioritise and Schedule your Critical Decisions
- when each wish has been assessed, rank them in order of priority
- discuss each of them in order of importance, rating their pros and cons
- choose the top five wishes and decide which is the most important, and when you want to purchase it, or do it

6 Decide on First Actions to Prepare for Most Important Decision
- when you have decided on a few major decisions, determine what actions to take to achieve them
- everyone in the family should have something to do with implementing the decision

7
Create this Year's Theme for your Family
- at the end of the meeting, or at another meeting, discuss the idea of an annual family theme
- get everyone to suggest possible themes, and choose one you all like
- use a Family Theme skillsheet to come up with activities related to the theme

8
Hold Regular Family Compact Meetings
- once you begin your family compact, it's important to hold regular meetings, either weekly or monthly
- these meetings can also be used to discuss other matters, not just those related to money

CHAPTER 15

Split Economies

---

3 MAJOR GOALS

1 To learn how to handle children and money issues raised by divorce or separation

2 To learn how to teach your children sound financial principles with or without the co-operation of your ex-spouse

3 To teach your children to compare different styles of money management

When parents separate or divorce, it's much more difficult to teach your kids about money. If you are in this situation, you have probably discovered the difficulties. Your ex-spouse may have a totally different way of dealing with money. In fact, your incompatibility about money may have contributed to the break-up of your marriage. In this case, teaching kids your values about money may seem next to impossible if they are learning the complete opposite values in their other household.

For example, you may want your kids to save their money for medium-term goals, while your ex-spouse gives them money whenever they want to buy something. If this is the case, a number of things can happen. Your kids may become confused. They may wonder: "Should I save my money, or go out and spend, spend, spend?" Your children might start to manipulate you, playing you off against their other parent. You may feel tempted to keep up with your ex-spouse or dole out treats and lavish gifts to, in fact, pay for your kids' affections. If you fall into this me-too trap, all of your good efforts up to now may be undermined. And more important, the mixed signals being sent to your children will confuse them, and make it harder for them to develop strong values about money.

On the other hand, divorce or separation does not need to spell the end of your kids' money management program. Although it may be harder to accomplish, it's still possible to teach your kids the lessons in this book, with or without the support of your ex-spouse. If you can get your ex-spouse to join forces with you, to help your children learn about money, that's great. If not, you can still set an excellent example for your kids, regardless of what is happening in the other household. In fact, you can help your children learn to identify and compare the different money styles in their two households. This comparison will help bring into sharp focus all of the values and lessons discussed in the book. But make every effort to do this in a non-judgmental way. Facts can be stated clearly and positively to provide understanding rather than criticism.

The key to teaching your kids about money in this situation is to use this book as your ultimate source. If you approach your ex-spouse about this issue, you can say the ideas come from this book, not from you. Using this book as the source of these ideas will deflect criticism away from you, and possibly change scepticism into curiosity. As well, if your children start to complain about how you handle money in your household, you can simply point to this book. In fact, I have no problem if you blame everything on me and my book. You can cast me as the evil taskmaster. Using this book instead of yourself as the source of the ideas means you don't have to take the rap for all the difficulties you have with your kids about money. Just blame it on the book, and then convince them to follow it too!

The Key Split Economies Principles

If your kids live part of the time in another household with your ex-spouse, teaching them about money is an extra challenge. However, if you observe these principles, you will have a better chance of success.

Split Economies Principle 1: **Try to forge a united front.**

Split Economies Principle 2: **Stick to your guns.**

Split Economies Principle 3: **Make the differences crystal clear.**

Split Economies Principle 4: **Don't compete with your ex-spouse.**

Split Economies Principle 5: **Beware of the over-compensation factor.**

Split Economies Principle 6: **Watch manipulation-to-the-max.**

Split Economies Principle 7: **Remember: love is more important than money.**

Split Economies Principle 8: **Lose battles, win the war.**

Try to Forge a United Front

Your first step should be to try to bring your ex-spouse on side with your kids and money program. I used the word "try" because it is not always possible. But you have to give your ex-spouse a chance to lend his or her support. I suggest you speak with them in person or by telephone, and tell them about how you are handling money with your kids. Explain The Allowance Contract, your approach to treats, savings, investing, big ticket items and other things you are doing. Find out if your ex-spouse is willing to develop a program which supports your ideas. If you get some resistance, try giving your ex-spouse this book to read, or buy them a copy. Use this book as the source of these ideas. If you sense some willingness to participate, start off slowly, perhaps by co-ordinating allowance.

If your ex-spouse is unwilling to go along with you, then let it go. Trying too hard to get your ex-spouse to participate in your program may simply inflame tensions, and ultimately harm your children. So be careful. Don't try too hard to sell these ideas, but it's important to give it a try.

SPLIT ECONOMIES PRINCIPLE 2
Stick to Your Guns

If you find your children are learning different money habits in their other household — and complaining to you about it — stick to your guns! Don't abandon your principles and values. Use the ideas in this book to support your efforts. Follow the step-by-step systems. Adhere to the principles. If you set a good example, even in the wake of bad examples, your lessons will get through eventually.

SPLIT ECONOMIES PRINCIPLE 3
Make the Differences Crystal Clear

When your children get confused about the conflicting money habits in each household, help them see the differences. Talk about how things are different in each house. Talk about why you do things the way you do. Perhaps the other household has two incomes while you have only one. Perhaps you believe in saving money for long-term goals, while the other family believes in spending money for today with a who-cares-about tomorrow attitude. The more distinct you can make the differences, the more likely your children will understand why you do things the way you do. As well, by pointing out the various ways people handle money, you will help your children to better appreciate the way you do things, and also to formulate their own unique relationship with the world of money.

SPLIT ECONOMIES PRINCIPLE 4
Don't Compete with your Ex-spouse

Whatever you do, don't start competing with your ex-spouse by trying to keep up with extravagant spending and lavish gifts. Such competition is a fool's game, and it can seriously harm your children. No matter what happens in the other household, you have to keep your wits about you. Don't try to match holiday for holiday, or treat for treat.

SPLIT ECONOMIES PRINCIPLE 5
Beware of the Over-compensation Factor

Many parents suffer tremendous guilt when they separate or divorce. They feel guilty that they can't be with their children every day, and worry that they're putting their own happiness ahead of their children. If this sounds like you, watch out. You might be trying to use money to mollify your guilt by lavishing treats and favours upon your children. This kind of over-compensation will undermine your kids' money management program. They may come to believe that money buys love.

SPLIT ECONOMIES PRINCIPLE 6
Watch Manipulation-to-the-Max

Children are very smart. And very crafty. They often figure out how to play one parent off against the other. (This phenomenon is not limited to divorced parents!) If you are feeling guilty or competitive, they will sniff it out a mile away. They'll play with your heartstrings, and all of a sudden you will be frantically doling out treats. So watch yourself, and watch your kids.

Are they trying to manipulate you? If so, nip this ploy in the bud. Call them on their little game. And stick to your guns. Don't be swayed.

SPLIT ECONOMIES PRINCIPLE 7

Remember: Love is More Important Than Money

If you stick to the principles and processes in this book, you will have much greater success teaching your kids that love is more important than money. Over time, your kids will realise you cared so much that you were willing to suffer their short-term disappointment and scorn for their long-term good.

SPLIT ECONOMIES PRINCIPLE 8

Lose Battles, Win the War

If you are battling against the different values being taught by your ex-spouse, take a more long-term perspective. Let go of the short term. Lose a few battles. Let your ex-spouse be the popular one. In fact, you might consider offering enthusiasm for what is happening at the other home. "That's great that you're going on a two-week vacation." "You're really lucky that your step-dad bought you new clothes." In my opinion, if you offer up support in this way, your kids will be more inclined to accept your way of doing things. So lose a few battles. You will likely win the war in the long run.

For Better and For Better

Although your marriage may have failed, you don't want to fail as a parent. It would be terrible if your kids didn't learn good money habits because their parents didn't get along. If possible, try to make some peace with your ex-spouse when it comes to teaching your kids about money. And by all means, don't use money as a way to compensate for guilt, or to compete with your ex-spouse. Take the high road. You'll be glad you did.

The Step-by-Step Systems

There are two step-by-step systems for Split Economies. The first process can be used if you can work together with your ex-spouse. The second process can be employed if co-operation is not possible or forthcoming.

System One: Co-operation

1 **Explain your Kids' Money Management Approach to your Ex-spouse**
If necessary, use this book as the central source of the concepts and principles. Have your ex-spouse read the book. Get him and her thinking along the same lines as you.

2 **Agree on a Common Approach to Allowance**
If your ex-spouse wants to play along, determine how much allowance to give, when it will be given, and who will give it. Also work out how much of the allowance will be saved, and where it will be deposited. You might consider giving allowance monthly to cut down on the confusion caused by going from one household to another.

System Two: Going It Alone

If you cannot rely on the co-operation of your ex-spouse, use this system:

1 **Set Your Own Ground Rules**
Tell your children the rules you have for money in your household. Use this book to lend authority to your ideas. Be very clear that you set the rules in your household, and your ex-spouse sets the rules in the other household.

2 **Answer Questions From your Children**
At this stage, it's important your children aren't confused by the different rules. Make sure they understand your rules and why you have them. Answer all of their questions.

3 **Discuss the Different Money Styles in Each Household**
Draw clear comparisons between your rules and the rules in the other household. Don't criticise the other way of doing things. Just point them out as different. Let the children make as many distinctions as possible without your prodding.

4 **Don't Buy into the "Big Bucks" Game**
If your ex-spouse is trying to one-up you with expensive trips and gifts, don't play the game. Stick to your principles. Whenever you feel you're going to start competing, or lose focus, come back to this book. Use it to keep you on track.

CHAPTER 16

Making Independent Choices

---
3 MAJOR GOALS

1 To teach your children how to make good choices independently

2 To teach your children how to set their own limits

3 To help your teenagers understand the risks and consequences of their choices

When kids enter their teens, everything changes. They go through physical changes, emotional changes and psychological changes. They're also called upon to take on more responsibility. To be more independent. To make their own choices. And a lot of these choices involve money.

These teen changes can be just as scary for you, the parent, as it is for your kids. You walk the very narrow path between imposing strict discipline (and choking their spirit and individuality), and giving them free rein (with possible negative and dangerous consequences). Obviously you will have different expectations and responsibilities for a 13-year-old than for a 19-year-old. But one principle to keep in mind is that once a privilege is given, it is much harder to change it or take it away. For example, if you don't give a curfew to a 14-year-old, but expect her to have common sense and come home around midnight, and she doesn't show up until 2:00 am, you are likely to be upset. And, to make matters worse, when you try to set a curfew for midnight, or even earlier, the teen is likely to be frustrated and uncooperative. Give privileges gradually, just as you have increased their allowances gradually.

The teen years can be challenging ones. But there is much potential for a satisfying outcome if you take the time to work with your teens to establish meaningful guidelines and provide them with positive support. The following principles should provide you with some material to work with.

The Key Independence Principles

When your teenagers start to flex their muscles of independence, you can use these principles to help you find the balance between being too strict and being too hands-off. Believe in your children. Show them that you have confidence in their ability to solve problems and make good choices. They need to feel your support at this tumultuous time of life, especially when they have made mistakes and are suffering the consequences.

Independence Principle 1: **Stand up for your values.**

Independence Principle 2: **Let kids make their own choices.**

Independence Principle 3: **Give guidance and offer good ideas.**

Independence Principle 4: **Don't substitute money for involvement.**

Independence Principle 5: **Create a sense of economic scarcity.**

Independence Principle 6: **Don't support bad habits.**

Independence Principle 7: **Establish clear guidelines.**

INDEPENDENCE PRINCIPLE 1
Stand Up for Your Values

No matter what values your kids try to adopt or defend, promote your own values. Show confidence in your value system. If your kids start smoking, and you don't like smoking in the house, don't allow it. You might not be able to get them to stop smoking (at least right away) but there's no reason to put up with smoke in your house because it affects your personal property. If you don't want your kids to wear clothes with controversial advertising or graphics, say so. But be ready to give your reasons why. By defending your personal boundaries, you will gain your kids' respect, and they will learn to articulate their own values. And by discussing the similarities and differences between your values, your kids will learn how to make better choices in their lives (even though their values may not always mesh with your own). Discussion promotes understanding, and is a valuable tool in relationships and in making money decisions. But be prepared to compromise, especially as your teens get older (e.g. rather than forbidding your teen to wear a certain T-shirt because you find it offensive, work out a compromise that you can both live with, such as only wearing the T-shirt while at home, not out in public). Barbara Coloroso, a well-known expert on parenting, reminds us *(Kids Are Worth It!*, Sumerville House Publishing, 1995, p.32) :

> If a situation is neither life-threatening, morally threatening, nor unhealthy, ask yourself if the natural consequence of what your child is doing would give life to your child's learning. If the answer is yes, stay out of it, and let nature take its course.

INDEPENDENCE PRINCIPLE 2
Let Kids Make their Own Choices

As your kids become older, and gradually more independent, let them make more and more of their own choices. Keeping in mind their age, experience and maturity, let them choose what they spend their money on, what things they do and what clothes they wear. You will likely put more limits on younger teens, but your goal is to have a confident 20-year-old who can handle his money responsibly. If you make these decisions for them, your kids will struggle to learn to make wise choices. And remember, you have to let them make mistakes. Mistakes are the best teachers of all. And when they make them, be sure to offer your understanding, and sometimes, your silence.

INDEPENDENCE PRINCIPLE 3
Give Guidance and Offer Good Ideas

Although you want your kids to make more of their own decisions, that doesn't mean you're out of the loop. Your job is to offer suggestions, advice and good ideas. You could suggest that instead of buying CDs, your kids borrow them from the library. Instead of going to a movie, they could invite their friends over to watch a video. Discuss the dangers of blowing money on things they don't really want or need, like excessive junk food, arcade games or make-up. Get involved. Give useful information. Leave pamphlets on health issues around the house. And then stand back.

INDEPENDENCE PRINCIPLE 4
Don't Substitute Money for Involvement

Some parents give their kids money, instead of time and effort. If kids start to see you, not as a role model, but as a source of ready cash, it's hard to get them to change their perspective. Set aside some time during the month to do something together that you both enjoy (or make it their choice) such as a lunch date, a sporting event, or an outdoor activity.

Slice of Life

Provide opportunities for your teens to talk to someone who has kicked a drug habit, or has had a bad experience. Teens need to hear stories first hand, rather than as a movie of the week scenario which seems irrelevant.

INDEPENDENCE PRINCIPLE 5
Create a Sense of Economic Scarcity

For your kids to develop a sense of financial responsibility, they must operate within an environment of economic scarcity. That means they have to feel there's a limit to how much money they can spend. Put them in a position where they have to make choices between one option and another (e.g. buying a new outfit or buying concert tickets).

Don't give your kids too much of their yearly budgeted allowance, just enough so they have to work if they want to buy fancy extras such as stereo systems, sports equipment and leather jackets. Once a month is a good time frame to provide money. This is similar to a regular pay cheque and provides a good routine.

Advertising tells us we need to have everything we want to be happy, so it's important to help our teens create goals and realistic expectations. Even if you are wealthy, it's a good idea to limit how much money your kids get for allowance. As long as your teen is a dependent (i.e. a student or unemployed), give them an allowance. But once they are independent, and are finished their education, expect them to support themselves. Paying parents for room and board is a reasonable expectation if a young adult is working full-time.

Slice of Life   Our eldest son wanted to buy a low rider bicycle (when they were a fad) from a friend for $40. I talked to him about the pros and cons, and then he decided to offer $20. His friend accepted the offer. After a month, the bike sat idle. Ryan then sold it for $10 — a $10 loss. It was a good learning experience for him.

INDEPENDENCE PRINCIPLE 6
Don't Support Bad Habits

If your kid wants to smoke or drink, he should have to pay for it himself. Some parents go out and buy the cigarettes for their kids. You might not be able to stop them from taking up bad habits, but you can refuse to be an accomplice and a source of cash. Tony Biglan, Ph.D., an expert on child and family psychology, stated in *Prevention Magazine* (January 1996, p. 92) that "kids who know that their parents give the thumbs-down to smoking are less likely to smoke than kids whose parents don't seem to care one way or another." Once again, defending your values sends a very powerful message.

Buying cigarettes for teens is a controversial issue for some. Concerns about teens stealing to supply their cigarettes, or paying older youth to buy for them may cause parents to buy the cigarettes themselves. Think carefully before doing this. Discuss the dangers and create solutions with your teen. Work for compromise.

INDEPENDENCE PRINCIPLE 7
Establish Clear Guidelines

Although you want your kids to spread their wings, you must provide guidelines. Make them simple, and clear, and make sure your teen understands them. They can cover such topics as house rules, property rules, curfew, school, car use and phone privileges. Spell out the consequences of straying from the guidelines. Make sure your teen acknowledges and accepts the rules and possible consequences.

Independence Tips & Traps

1. Get your kids to deposit pay cheques in the bank, and take out regular weekly amounts. They shouldn't cash the cheque and carry around large sums in their pocket.

2. Help your kids set up a weekly budget. Figure out how much they want to withdraw each week. Explain why they shouldn't take out any more money until the next week. You need to help them avoid dipping into their bank account every time they want something.

3. Encourage your kids to avoid hanging out at the mall or convenience stores unless they know exactly what they want to buy. The problem with window shopping is the impulse to buy.

4. Tell your kids to watch out for bullies who might want to steal their money. Convince them that the best defence is to carry only a minimum amount of money in their wallet.

5. Discourage your kids from borrowing from, or lending to, friends.

6. If your kids start hanging around with a new group of friends, find out what's going on. Get information. Talk to your kids about

their new friends. Invite their new friends to your home. Find out what they spend their money on, and where they get their money. Hopefully, this kind of engagement will help you prevent your kids from straying too far down the wrong path as you can use the information as a topic of discussion.

7. If your kids want to go to concerts with friends, be sure to explain the cost and safety issues involved. Get them to pay for the tickets. See if an older young adult can go with them, or arrange for a large group of kids to go together.

8. Set limits on dating. It is an important part of teenage life, but too often teens are not given much guidance when they start to date. Help your teen make sensible choices regarding the cost of dates, gifts and activities.

9. If you suspect your child may have a drug or alcohol dependence, don't hesitate to get help. Sneaking or stealing money from parents is a strong signal that something is wrong. Look for a well-recommended professional to help. Check out a self-help program such as Al-anon for yourself, and your teen or speak with your family doctor about options. Don't make the mistake of thinking that it is just a stage that will soon pass.

Slice of Life

Clients I know have saved the room and board money they charged their working teens so that there were savings available for loans if their teen needed one, or for a down payment for a townhouse or a car.

The Step-by-Step System

1   Discuss your values with your teenagers.

2   Have your teenagers discuss what they believe in.

3   Discuss the difference in your values.

4   Set limits and guidelines based on the discussion.

5   Establish an appropriate allowance and review it as your child ages.

6   Have your teenagers set a weekly budget.

7   Have your kids deposit their pay cheques directly in the bank.

8   Offer advice and ideas when appropriate.

9   Let your kids make their own choices.

10   Discuss the results of those choices with your kids when appropriate.

CHAPTER 17

Marketing Madness

3 MAJOR GOALS

1 To teach your children how advertising and other marketing can influence their buying decisions

2 To teach your children to set their own limits on buying "cool" brand name stuff

3 To help them get some of the "cool" stuff they want without spending a fortune

As a parent, I've often felt powerless against the sophisticated and powerful marketers who target their cross-media ad campaigns directly at my kids. Wherever my kids and I look — TV, movies, the video store, magazines, radio, Internet, billboards and even sky-high blimps — we are exposed to slick and co-ordinated marketing campaigns. And the message is simple: "The more you buy, the better you'll feel." The marketers are trying to get our kids to believe their self-worth is directly tied to the type of clothes they wear, the kind of music they listen to, and the kind of sports equipment they use. And these marketing-to-youth campaigns are not limited to clothes and music; they are also being used by liquor and tobacco companies to hook your kids while they're in their teens.

So, as a parent, what can you do to share your values with your kids in the face of this media barrage? Well, you could do nothing, and let your kids sort it all out. But that's a dangerous strategy. If you do nothing, your kids may never become aware of the effect this marketing madness has upon their self-image and upon their buying habits. They may grow up taking their cues from television commercials, radio ads and websites. They may never learn how to become smart, confident shoppers. Your kids may become shopaholics, hanging out in shopping malls, spending all of their money the moment they get it. But worst of all, they may adopt the wrong kind of values: values which serve the interest of marketers, not the well being of your children. They may define themselves using the criteria set out by advertising firms and marketing departments. And they may never learn to ask themselves what is good and meaningful.

But there is hope. You can help your children avoid marketing madness, and learn how to become sophisticated consumers. It just takes a little work and commitment on your part. If you follow the principles and the step-by-step system in this chapter, you have the opportunity to teach your kids:

- how to sort through marketing hype to find useful information;
- how marketers are trying to influence them (in both positive and negative ways);
- how we are adversely affected by certain kinds of advertising;
- how to judge for themselves what products and services are useful and valuable, and what are not needed;
- how to become savvy consumers;
- how to get what they want — the "cool" stuff — without wasting their money.

Most important, your kids will learn to be more independent: less under the influence of marketers, and more independent of you as well. If the marketers get to your kids, they are going to come to you looking for more money or to ask you to buy them something totally outrageous. So it's important to realise that you not only need to save your kids from marketing madness, you have to save yourself.

The Key Marketing Principles

To teach your kids how to avoid marketing madness and think for themselves as smart and sophisticated consumers, the following principles will help.

Marketing Principle 1: **Discuss marketing madness with your kids.**

Marketing Principle 2: **Teach your kids how to spot marketing madness when they see it.**

Marketing Principle 3: **Support your child's need to fit in.**

Marketing Principle 4: **Explain the cost of being "cool".**

Marketing Principle 5: **Set limits on name brand purchases.**

Marketing Principle 6: **Discourage window shopping.**

Marketing Principle 7: **Avoid special sales days and events.**

Marketing Principle 8: **Teach smart consumer habits.**

Marketing Principle 9: **Explain the safety issues of being "cool."**

Marketing Principle 10: **Cut down on exposure to marketing hype.**

MARKETING PRINCIPLE 1

Discuss Marketing Madness With your Kids

To help your kids overcome the often hidden influence of marketers on our lives, the first step is to bring the issue to the forefront. Talk with your kids about marketing madness. Explain that:

- advertising and other promotions are used to make you think a certain way;
- advertising can be really useful because it can help you find the things you need at a really good price;
- sometimes advertising makes you want things which you don't really need;

- sometimes advertising makes you want things which are bad for you (i.e. cigarettes);
- sometimes advertising makes things look better than they really are;
- sometimes advertising doesn't tell the whole truth.

In addition to talking about advertising and other marketing tools, discuss with your kids how brand names such as designer labels are used to get you to spend more money than a product is worth. You are, in fact, simply paying extra to be "cool."

MARKETING PRINCIPLE 2

Teach your Kids How to Spot Marketing Madness When they See It

The best way to "media train" your kids is to look at advertising together. Look at print and television ads and ask your kids:

- What do you think the advertiser is trying to tell you?
- What do you think the advertiser is trying to get you to think?
- What do you think the advertiser is trying to get you to do?
- How does the ad make you feel? What do you want to do after seeing this ad?
- Do you think the product is as good as the ad says it is?

By looking at advertising in this critical way, you will teach your kids to size up the hype factor. You might also learn a thing or two about your own attitudes toward advertising and marketing madness.

MARKETING PRINCIPLE 3
Support your Children's Need to Fit In

When you were a teenager, you probably wanted to be popular, to fit in. Well, your kids are no different. To be confident, they need to feel accepted. They need to wear the right clothes and do the right things. It's perfectly natural. Being part of a group is one of our most human needs. So don't try to quash their need or ridicule it. Talk about it. Be supportive. Help your kids get what they need to be part of the group, without spending a fortune.

MARKETING PRINCIPLE 4
Explain the Costs of Being "Cool"

While supporting your kids' need to be "cool," you can still help them see the costs associated with trying to be popular by wearing certain kinds of clothing. From a purely financial standpoint, your kids can learn that name brand jeans are more expensive than non-name-brand jeans even though they are virtually identical. So while you are supporting some of your kids' I-need-to-be-"cool" activities, make sure you have a discussion with them about the costs. It might sink in.

MARKETING PRINCIPLE 5
Set Limits on Name Brand Purchases

The best way to get your kids to understand the costs of being "cool" is to set a limit on how much you will contribute to any particular purchase. For example, if your child needs new running shoes, agree to contribute $75 to the purchase. Anything beyond that amount must be covered with his own money. In this way, your kids will have to make the choice to spend more money on a pair of extra-expensive running shoes. They will have to think twice whether it's worth it or not.

MARKETING PRINCIPLE 6
Discourage Window Shopping

One of the reasons people spend too much money on things they don't need is because they go window shopping. They wander from store to store, through malls, from website to website. Sooner or later they are gripped by the impulse to buy a toaster cover or a doggy sweater — things they would never deliberately go out to buy and probably don't need. So discourage window shopping. Don't let your kids hang out at the mall as if it's a community centre. Don't take them out "shopping" just for the fun of it.

MARKETING PRINCIPLE 7
Avoid Special Sales Days and Events

Discourage your kids from shopping on Boxing Day or in stores holding midnight madness sales, hoping for a great deal. Explain that people buy all kinds of things they don't really want at these sales. A kind of frenzy takes hold. People start clutching and grabbing at the merchandise. Of course, your kids will probably go anyway just to see what's so great about the midnight sale, but at least they'll go in with a little more scepticism.

MARKETING PRINCIPLE 8
Teach Smart Consumer Habits

There are several habits which effectively combat the ravages of marketing madness. To help your kids be smart consumers, teach them to:

- Have a purchase in mind before heading out to a store or the mall;
- Look at flyers and advertising to find what they want at the lowest possible price;
- Go to factory outlets to get low prices on name brand products (however, keep in mind that factory outlet malls are marketing madness in the extreme);
- Phone or go to a number of stores before they finally buy;
- Ask about the warranty before they buy;
- Keep the receipts for every purchase so they can return the product if it is not satisfactory.

MARKETING PRINCIPLE 9
Explain the Safety Issues of Being "Cool"

In some schools and communities, it can be dangerous to be decked out in the latest designer duds. If your child is wearing the latest name brand fashions, she is a walking billboard shouting: "Steal from me, steal from me!" In many instances, kids have been robbed of leather jackets, jewellery, sports equipment, portable stereo equipment, and other expensive stuff. You need to teach your kids that conspicuous consumption in today's world can be risky. Try not to scare your kids too much, but do tell them the risks. In fact, you will probably discover your kids are more street savvy than you are. They'll likely understand exactly what you're talking about.

MARKETING PRINCIPLE 10

Cut Down on Exposure to Marketing Hype

Another weapon against media hype is abstention. Expose yourself and your kids to less media madness by turning off the television and radio. Avoid overly commercialised magazines and tabloids. Limit Internet use to non-commercial websites. Turn off and tune out. You won't be able to stem all of the tide, but you might slow it down a little.

Making Sense of Madness

As we all know, many of today's marketers have your kids in their sights. They know children have significant amounts of cash available and that they influence their parents' (and other adults') decisions. They'll do anything to persuade your kids to buy their products. So you have to fight back. Don't let your kids fend for themselves in today's media-saturated society. By making them aware of the up-sides and down-sides of the marketing world, you will help your kids make their own decisions, and become knowledgeable and skilled consumers.

The Step-by-Step System

Your goal in this process is to teach your kids to be smart consumers and to avoid marketing madness. Here's a step-by-step system I've found works well with my family.

Review Advertising With your Kids
Take a look at advertising in newspapers and magazines. Discuss what the advertis-

ers are trying to make you think and feel. Critique television ads with your kids. Raise your kids' awareness that some marketers use advertising to make you want things you don't really need.

2   **Rate the Ads and Commercials**
Rate the advertising you review from one to 10. Ten is for commercials which provide good information about a useful product or service. One is for commercials which use flashy graphics and broad statements to entice you into buying something frivolous or unnecessary.

3   **Find Out What Stuff your Kids Like**
As I've said, you should try to support your kids' need to be "cool." So when you are looking at advertising, find out what brand names are all the rage. At least if you are forewarned, you will be forearmed.

4   **Talk to Other Parents**
Other parents will have lots of ideas on what kids want these days. Speak to them. Share information.

5   **Set Limits on How Much You'll Contribute for Trendy Brand Names**
Decide on a pre-set amount of money to give your child to buy a particular item. If they want a more trendy version, let them top up your contribution. Then they'll have to think carefully about whether they really want to buy it. For example, when we go shopping for running shoes for the

guys, we decide on a price we're willing to pay for a shoe before we go shopping. Our kids know that if they see a super sneaker that costs $120, they will have to pay for any amount above our set limit. Usually, they are amazingly satisfied with a sale-priced brand name shoe.

6 **Set a General Spending Budget**
Before you go out shopping with your kids, set up a budget. State how much you are willing to contribute to new clothes. Determine together what clothes are actually needed. As I've said, your child can then add to your funds if they want to buy the latest trends. Their money can come from their short- or medium-term savings.

7 **Use Catalogues, Flyers and Consumer Reports**
Have your children do their homework. Teach them that you can often find great deals just by looking through all of the different ads.

8 **Have a Specific Purchase in Mind Before Heading to the Mall**
Don't go window shopping. Don't hang around the mall all day. Avoid impulse purchases.

9

Go to Different Shops to Find the Best Deals

When you go out looking for a specific product, shop around. Take your kids to at least two stores before making their purchase. The experience will teach them that they can often find a better deal by looking around.

CHAPTER 18

To Be or Not To Be "In"

3 MAJOR GOALS

1 To teach your children to recognise the dangers of always trying to keep up with the "cool" kids

2 To teach your children how to increase their confidence without always spending money or buying things

3 To teach your children how to decide if they really want to spend money just to fit "in" with their friends

Being part of the "cool" crowd is one of the primary concerns of just about every child. But this need to belong becomes especially acute when kids enter high school. The pressure to conform is enormous. You are either "in" or you're "out," and usually the way to be "in" is to wear the right clothes, own the right stuff, and do the "cool" things. In other words, if you want to be "in" you've got to spend money — lots of it — on designer clothes, cool hairstyles, trendy restaurants, arcades, concerts, movies, and other less desirable things such as cigarettes, beer and drugs. The US Surgeon General's report on tobacco and teens found that "nicotine is generally the first drug used by young people who use alcohol, marijuana and harder drugs. Most of today's smokers picked up their first cigarette before age fifteen."

When your children reach their teenage years, they will probably try to use money and consumer products to help them join the "in" crowd. Why? Because owning the right stuff and doing the right things can bolster their confidence and their self-esteem. And I'm not just talking about kids. I'm talking about you and me. Inside all of us is the desire to keep up with the Joneses; to own a better car, or to buy a bigger house. It's a natural instinct. Unfortunately, it becomes a serious problem when trying to be "in" turns into an obsession. In this case, keeping up or trying to belong distorts your reality, your values and your choices. And from a financial standpoint, it can be disastrous.

So it's very likely your kids will come to you looking for more money when they reach their teens, because trying to be "cool" is expensive. When this happens, you could be in big trouble if you don't have a plan. If you refuse to support your kids' need to belong, they could rebel against you. You could become the bad guy. It could ruin your relationship with them. And if you clamp down too hard, you could seriously harm their self-esteem. They could feel like an outcast at school. However, if you just give them money, your kids may learn the wrong lessons. They may start to equate their self-worth with how much they own. They may adopt very shallow, consumer-oriented values and spend the rest of their lives trying to match or better their neighbours' purchases. If they don't learn how to bolster their self-confidence in non-monetary ways, they may adopt some of the more dangerous in-crowd habits such as smoking cigarettes or taking drugs. As well, all of their good money habits, which they've spent years developing, may vanish in a frenzy of shopping and merry-making, leaving them with no cash to maintain the image or the hype.

On the other hand, this situation also presents a splendid opportunity for you. You can help your kids to recognise the dangers of spending money just to be part of the crowd. You can help them develop the confidence to say "no" to peer pressure when it's not appropriate. You can also teach them to make choices based on their own values, not those of the gang at school. As well, they could come to see you as a partner, not an adversary. You could be someone who will help them be "cool" to some degree while still insisting that some limits be observed.

Fortunately, if your kids have developed sound money habits, it's likely they will already have the confidence, and the structure to handle peer pressure more effectively. They have learned to make choices.

| Slice of Life | CD's are expensive and "cool" for only a short time. The library is a great place to borrow CDs to play for a week or two at a time. |

The Key Cool Principles

When your kids want to be "cool," they will want more money. Chances are they will come to you looking for it. If this happens, follow these principles:

Cool Principle 1: **Support your kids' need to be "in."**
Cool Principle 2: **Support non-consumer ways to belong.**
Cool Principle 3: **Set limits on your contributions to the "cool" campaign.**
Cool Principle 4: **Create a Teen Purchase Plan.**
Cool Principle 5: **Teach your kids to make a shopping list.**
Cool Principle 6: **Let your kids do their own shopping.**
Cool Principle 7: **Discuss the pros and cons of the "in crowd" mentality.**

COOL PRINCIPLE 1

Support your Kids' Need to Be "In"

Being cool is part of growing up. It instils confidence and builds self-esteem. If you don't support this need, both financially and emotionally, your kids could rebel, or find other ways to get the support they need: sometimes with the wrong people. So it's important to support their need to be part of a group of friends. Offer understanding and some financial support. The key word in that last sentence is "some." Give your children some help in getting the cool things they need. Share the expense, don't take on all of it.

| Slice of Life | Clothing that advertises any alcohol or tobacco names should be avoided. These are powerful value statements. |

COOL PRINCIPLE 2

Support Non-consumer Ways to Belong

There are many ways to feel part of a group without spending exorbitant sums of money on the latest fashions or the coolest concerts. You can encourage your kids to join sports teams, hobby clubs, scholastic clubs, church groups, or volunteer committees. Instead of giving them money to spend at the mall, help them join and participate in positive groups. You might find they won't want to spend as much money on consumer goods if they're busy having fun with friends in these groups. For example, instead of taking their kids off to a movie, one family we know invites a number of friends over for a movie night. They provide the movie and the popcorn, and the guests are encouraged to bring drinks or snacks.

COOL PRINCIPLE 3

Set Limits on your Contributions to the "Cool" Campaign

If your kids are hell-bent on being consumer maniacs, you've got to set limits on your personal contributions to their habit. Agree to contribute a certain amount to buy consumer goods and to participate in activities, but make them pay for the rest. Set a low enough limit on your contribution that they will truly feel the pain of paying for being cool. As well, make sure you direct your money to specific purchases or activities. To maintain some control over the process, you can give them gift certificates earmarked for specific purposes. Whatever, you do, don't give them carte blanche with a credit or debit card. You will pay for the rest of your life!

COOL PRINCIPLE 4
Create a Teen Purchase Plan

One way to help your kids avoid the in-crowd trap is to help them develop a purchase plan. If you and your kids plan out purchases in advance, they will be less likely to buy something on impulse or because they simply recognise the brand name. During the preparation of the plan, you can discuss what your kids want to buy, and why they want to buy it. Is it because they really need it, or is it because their best friend has the same thing? Calculate the money needed annually and then pay the teen monthly or by item. This money is given in addition to their regular allowance, and represents the money you would normally have spent to purchase their annual needs (such as shoes, coats, clothing and toiletry items).

See the Teenage Purchase Plan I have created in The Skillsheets section at the back of this book or create your own. You need to outline what items your teen wants to purchase, the cost and the amount contributed by parents and/or your teenager.

COOL PRINCIPLE 5
Teach your Kids to Make a Shopping List

Before your kids go out shopping, help them make up a list of what they need to buy with the money they have available. For example, let's say your kid has $2.50 to spend. Make it clear that the money is to cover the cost of two pairs of pants, three shirts, underwear and socks. Blowing the whole amount on a cool jacket is not on the list! Create a Shopping Planner* skillsheet

---

*I have created a Shopping Planner Skillsheet and it is available at www.makingallowances.com.

which outlines your child's research on what he wants to buy, where and for how much.

COOL PRINCIPLE 6

Let your Kids Do their Own Shopping

If your kids have a purchase plan, and you've set some clear limits on your contribution, and have discussed their needs, it's a good idea to let them do their own shopping. Older teens need to experience buying their own stuff, using their own money. Of course, this doesn't mean you don't get involved to some degree. You can still offer advice, and go with them if you feel they want help. However, you should let them buy what they want, as long as they get what they need on the shopping list within the budget. And if they don't, make allowances for their choices (after you've counted to 10 and stopped yourself from giving a lecture!) but DO NOT go out and buy the items they should have bought. They will have to wait until the next allowance or pay cheque.

COOL PRINCIPLE 7

Discuss the Pros and Cons of the "In Crowd" Mentality

It's very important for you to listen and discuss this issue with your teenage children. They must feel you understand their need to be cool, while conversely, they need to appreciate the limits of your participation. It's also important to highlight the reasons why people use money and material possessions to bolster their ego, and why it can be a very dangerous game to play. We all know adults who have new cars owned by the bank, and credit cards charged to the max trying to maintain a certain look or lifestyle.

So "In," It's "Out"

When your kids grow up, they will either live their life by their own rules, or by rules set by others. If they choose the latter, the rules might not be in their best interest. They may spend the rest of their lives trying to be someone they're not — always striving for the bigger boat or the more expensive shoes. I hope the principles and systems discussed in this chapter will help you teach your children how to make their own rules, how to live by their own values and how to find personal confidence without the approval of the "in" crowd.

The Step-by-Step System

Your objective is to help your kids develop self-esteem, confidence, a sense of control and a feeling of community without always using money or consumer goods to be cool. This step-by-step system will help you teach your kids less consumer-oriented values, and help reinforce the good money habits they've adopted up to now.

1 Discuss the Pros and Cons of Trying to be "In"

Sit down with your kids and talk about their need to be a member of a group. Discuss what they need to do and own to feel part of the group. Work together to decide how much it's worth in money to be part of the "in" crowd.

2 Create a Budget

Use the Teenage Purchase Plan skillsheet to create a budget for each child. Decide how much you are willing to contribute, and how much they will contribute. Make your limit, and the reason for it, very clear. This can clarify for your teens the real cost of a certain lifestyle, and what choices they need to make (i.e. buy concert tickets or buy a CD).

3 Create a Shopping List
Before your children head out to the stores, help them make a shopping list. Encourage them to purchase everything on the list for the set budget. Revise the list or budget if necessary. Reinforce positive choices.

4 Review Ads, Flyers and Catalogues
As much as possible, use advertising and catalogues to look for different brands and prices. When you find a good deal, write down the name of the store on the shopping list. Look for real sales!

5 Go Shopping With your Children
The first time they go shopping, you should go along. Offer suggestions and help them stay within their budget. However, don't meddle in their ultimate decisions. If they want to buy pink trousers, a lime green sweater, and a boa hat, just nod your head and carry on. Try to remember when you wore outrageous clothes. At the mall, you might split up and meet later to encourage decision making and confidence in their choices.

6 Review the Purchases
Following the shopping excursion, go over the list. Did they get everything they

planned to get? Was the budget too low, or too high? Did they find any good bargains? Are they happy with the merchandise? What items were missed or need to be looked for in future sales?

7 **Stress the Importance of Long-Term Care**
At this point, it's a good opportunity to talk to your kids about how to look after their possessions. Talk about regular cleaning and maintenance. Discuss warranties and returns. Ask them to commit to look after their stuff. If they insist on buying clothes that must be dry-cleaned, make that their responsibility. Again this is a powerful lesson in choices and is not about you being mean.

In this section, we have concentrated on buying clothes and other products. However, the process is also applicable to other activities. For example, you might want to help your children develop a year-long budget for concerts, movies, restaurants, car-related expenses and other similar expenses. In this case, you can also determine the limit of your contribution. The most important thing is to give your children the time and structure to think through their buying decisions beforehand.

Using the Teen Cash Flow skillsheet from The Skillsheets section is an opportunity to have your teen look at the overall cash flow requirements for a year. What will their allowance be used for? How much will be allotted for their annual expenditures on clothing, etc.? What are the costs of operating a car and who will pay for the insurance, gas, maintenance, etc.? Reviewing beforehand and setting limits on your contribution will give your teen the information to help make good choices. (Part-time jobs become popular!)

CHAPTER 19

The Lifetime Goal Formula

3 MAJOR GOALS

1 To teach your children how to set lifetime goals

2 To give your children the confidence to strive for their goals

3 To help your children identify their true instincts, abilities and passions

It's accepted wisdom that goal-setting is the corner-stone of sound financial planning. By planning ahead, it's much easier to forego immediate gratification and avoid spur-of-the-moment mistakes. If your kids have been diligently working with you on the concepts in this book, they are probably getting good at setting goals for themselves — not just financial goals, but life goals as well. In this final chapter, I wish to help you teach your kids how to make goal-setting a regular habit. I believe this skill, above all else, will help your kids live more successful lives, financially and other-wise.

Why do I put such an emphasis on goal-setting? Well, I've seen what happens when kids aren't interested in their future. Lacking direction, they often become depressed. They exhibit a sense of hopelessness. Without a vision of an exciting and positive future, they don't care about themselves or other people. Kids without goals tend to dart from one activity to anoth-er, never spending adequate time on anything to get a sense of accomplishment. Teenagers who don't set goals for themselves tend to live only for today, never saving or investing in their future. Hence, these kids may flounder for a long time before figuring out what they really want for their future and becoming suc-cessful citizens.

On the flip side, kids who set goals, and achieve them, see the world from a totally different perspective. They know their futures will be positive. They know they can achieve anything they want if they put their minds to it and work hard. They exude confidence and an aura of maturity. By engaging in lots of activi-ties, and by testing themselves in many different situations, kids with goals know themselves better. They know what they like to do, and what they're passionate about. They're well-prepared to choose their own paths to a bright future. And finally, kids who know how to set goals are much more likely to achieve success. Always looking ahead, they save money rather than wasting it on superficial pleasures.

If you want your kids to resemble the latter rather than the former, teach them how to set goals. Get them hooked on the habit, and you'll be amazed at the difference. The following principles will help you to teach your kids to set goals.

The Key Goal Principles

Helping your kids set goals is an exciting process. It's my hope parents will adopt and act upon these very simple principles along side their children.

Goal Principle 1: **Encourage active dreaming.**

Goal Principle 2: **Let your kids pick their own future.**

Goal Principle 3: **Expose your kids to lots of options.**

Goal Principle 4: **Support their unique talents and passions.**

Goal Principle 5: **Monitor progress and celebrate achievements.**

Goal Principle 6: **Provide opportunities and limits for activities.**

Goal Principle 7: **Talk about goal-setting at the appropriate time.**

Goal Principle 8: **Don't just set goals, teach goal-setting skills.**

GOAL PRINCIPLE 1

Encourage Active Dreaming

Every great achievement begins with a dream. So encourage your kids to talk about what they want to do in the future. Let them brainstorm out loud about all the terrific places they'd like to visit, the kinds of jobs they'd like to have and the activities they'd like to engage in. Don't judge their dreams or assess their practicality. Let them go wild with their ideas. Teach them to not be discouraged by those who belittle or disregard their dreams. Encourage your kids to make dreaming a regular part of life. Like I said, everything great usually starts with a dream.

GOAL PRINCIPLE 2

Let your Kids Pick Their Own Future

Most of us want our kids to be successful, and perhaps to fulfil some of the dreams we have been unable to achieve. It's a natural instinct, but a dangerous one. In most cases, our kids have different personalities, instincts, talents and interests. If we try to force them to follow a path of our choosing, they'll end up discouraged, unhappy and bitter. So let your kids pick their own future. Let them do it their way, not your way. Sure, you can offer advice and support. But keep it at arms length. Allow them to participate in activities they wish to enjoy and learn from. As I've said throughout this book, making allowances means letting your kids set their own course, with guidance from you.

Slice of Life | I find talking to my boys while driving to one of their activities is a great opportunity to talk and ask questions. Little moments throughout the month allow me to stay in touch with what is going on in their thoughts, and in their lives.

GOAL PRINCIPLE 3
Expose your Kids to Lots of Options

The more your kids know about the world, the more they will learn about themselves. To help your kids make good choices about their future, expose them to new people, new ideas and lots of new experiences. Talk with them about the jobs other people do. Encourage them to speak with friends and relatives about their jobs. Take them to factories and offices. If you know people who are successful in their work, have your kids meet them. Use them as role models. Talk to your kids about the lifestyle they would like to have, and the cash flow needed to support that lifestyle. As well, encourage your kids to read books by successful and authoritative authors including those in the Other Resources section at the back of this book. And most of all, let them participate in an abundance of activities. The more they do, the more confident they'll become.

GOAL PRINCIPLE 4
Support their Unique Talents and Passions

If you see that your kids have a passion for a particular hobby or field of interest, offer as much support as possible for it. If they love doing something, it's likely it's the thing they should focus on. To help you discover your kids' unique talents and strengths, I encourage you to use one of the many excellent "character profile" indexes. One index which I have used to great success is the one developed by Kathy Kolbe from Phoenix, Arizona. The Kolbe Index, suitable for children at the fifth grade reading level and up, will help you and your kids identify their unique instincts, and help you direct them where their passions can make them truly successful and fulfilled. See the Other Resources section at the end of this book for more information.

Monitor Progress and Celebrate Achievements

Perfectionism is one danger of setting goals. When people become goal-oriented, they often forget to celebrate their achievements. They may be miserable, no matter what success they've had — for example, when winning, second or third place is not celebrated. To avoid this pitfall, help your kids learn to appreciate each step along the way. Talk with them about their progress. What accomplishment did they make today? How do they feel about it?

Using a Lifetime Goal Formula* skillsheet or your own list of one-month, one-year, three-year and life-time goals, your kids can write down the goals they want to achieve in their life. Do they want to travel the world, own their own company, win an Academy Award, or have a big family? What other goals do they have? When they have these lifetime goals written down, work backwards. What goals do they need to have for the next three years, one year, one month? This exercise is excellent because it helps your kids see a direct path to their future. It instils the idea that even the biggest goals can be achieved one day at a time. Review these goals with your child quarterly, semi-annually and annually (or even as often as monthly with your teens).

Your kids can build confidence in a powerful way by looking at their achievements on the Powerful

---

*I have created The Big Dreams Formula Skillsheet and it is available at www.makingallowances.com.

Achievement Formula skillsheet.* Each night before bedtime, ask your children about one accomplishment or achievement they made that day, whatever they might be. Examples could include finishing a book, doing a good deed for someone, completing a chore the child hates, doing well in class that day, drawing a great picture, or having a good practice. After the first month, start to write down their daily achievement in a journal (older kids can write it themselves). Then after another month, together, write down two or three more achievements each night. After only a few weeks, kids seem to look upon life with a more positive attitude and with a keen sense of achievement. It's really a simple exercise, and yet the results are remarkable. I highly recommend it. Also, don't let your ideas of what achievements are important direct your child's answers. Listen to your child and learn — you'll be surprised and encouraged.

GOAL PRINCIPLE 6
Provide Opportunities and Limits for Activities

When your kids decide they want to pursue a hobby or an activity, lend your moral and financial support, with one major condition. If your child wants to learn how to play the guitar, or take ballet lessons, they have to be prepared to stick it out for at least one or two years. They shouldn't get in the habit of flitting from this to that, dropping out whenever things get too hard or too frustrating. So make the deal. If you are going to pay for them to learn judo or landscape painting, they have to sign on for the duration.

---

*I have created a the Powerful Achievement Formula Skillsheet and it is available at www.makingallowances.com.

A great way to experience many activities without a long-term commitment or high cost is by taking classes through your local community centre or college. Encourage your kids to try new things this way. The final decisions of how many activities to participate in, and how much the family can afford will be decided by the parents. But make sure your kids are able to give input. Try to keep the number of activities reasonable, based on the child's temperament, and parental availability and financial obligations.

GOAL PRINCIPLE 7

Talk About Goal-Setting at the Appropriate Time

There is a right time, and a wrong time, to speak to your kids about their "future." Ideally, broach this subject when you're relaxed and when there won't be a lot of distractions. If you pick the wrong time, your kids might think you are pestering them. They might never get around to talking to you about their goals because they'll think it isn't "cool." So use your good judgement. Pick your moments carefully.

GOAL PRINCIPLE 8

Don't Just Set Goals, Teach Goal-Setting Skills

You want to teach your kids how to set goals on their own, not just help them set some goals with your direction. It's an important distinction. Help them develop the habit of looking at their lives from a future-based perspective. Show them how to write down their goals, and the actions required to achieve them. Teach them how to celebrate the achievement of their progress toward their long-term goals.

It's the Goal-Setting, Not the Goals

When you're helping your kids set lifetime goals, remember that it's not important if they achieve those exact goals, it's the confidence they develop from dreaming big dreams. Setting goals gives a person confidence, and adds excitement to our day-to-day existence. So have fun with your kids. Don't worry so much about achieving every goal. Just enjoy taking the trip, no matter where the journey takes you and your kids.

The Step-by-Step System

1 **Expose your Kids to Lots of Different Activities**
Get them involved in a variety of areas including sports, music, theatre, and other hobbies. The more they experience, the more they'll learn about themselves.

2 **Take a Character Profile Index**
Help your children discover their unique talents and strengths.

3 **Discuss the Work Situation of Friends and Relatives**
Talk to your kids about what other people do for a living. Explain what the job is like, what's good and what's bad about it. Talk about the type of lifestyle they enjoy.

4 **Offer your Kids Great Books by Great Authors**
Reading is one of the best ways for kids to explore new ideas and learn valuable lessons from the great masters. See the

Other Resources section at the back of this book for a detailed list of books and authors.

5 **Do the Lifetime Goals Exercise**
Ask your kids to write down the things they want to achieve in their life. Then work backwards. Have them write down what they want to accomplish in three years, one year and one month. A fun and interesting activity is for your kids to describe their dreams and goals by making a poster, a collage of magazine clippings, a timeline or a cartoon.

6 **Do the Powerful Achievement Exercise**
In this exercise, at the end of each day, your kids write down (or verbalise) what they accomplished during that day. They write down why it was important and what further progress they want to make? This helps solidify their sense of confidence and achievement. If you think completing this exercise daily may be overdoing it, do it once a week, or perhaps from Sunday through Thursday, which our family does.

In Conclusion

Time and experience have shown us that money, or the lack of it, can be the root of much conflict in our lives. The debt trap is deep, so easy to sink into, and so hard to climb out of. Not having the proper education and structure to rely on can leave young people in a difficult position.

A recent story in a national newspaper showcased a young man in his early twenties who is struggling with financial problems. The story chronicled his plan to get a good job, buy a car, take some college courses and generally live the good life. The beginning of his troubles, however, began with an application for a credit card. After receiving credit, this young man believed that he could suddenly afford some things he hadn't considered before. He decided to buy some consumer goods. He applied for a student loan and went back to school. Four years later he is frequently hounded by a collection agency and burdened by payments he can barely cover, with little hope of paying off the debt he so easily took on. This young man is certainly not alone ... and his story underlines the importance of training young people to handle their finances responsibly. This young man is not stupid, underprivileged or uneducated. He is a statistic — representative of financial difficulties that many of us experience.

My hope is that your children will not find themselves in this unfortunate situation. I believe that with parental support, education, and practical skills like the ones presented in this book, they can become successful, financially responsible adults. As you help your children develop their own positive, confident value systems (including a commitment to community involvement and a charitable lifestyle), I am sure that you will be delighted with the financially independent and successful young adults that you launch into society. Children need hope: hope that their future will be bright, hope that their lives will have meaning, hope that they can make a positive difference in their world. You can help give your children hope for the future. Make allowances for their mistakes, provide them with a solid foundation, and enjoy the great adventure as you raise your children to have both dollars and sense.

THE SKILLSHEETS

Use the following skillsheets to work through the suggested exercises in this book. Make copies as you need them or download fresh copies from my Website at www.makingallowances.com.

The Allowance Contract

(Child) I, _____ will:
- receive $ _____ allowance every Sunday/Monday
- put _____% of allowance away for savings
- visit the bank on the last Saturday of every month to deposit savings
- retrieve savings only after it reaches a minimum of $ _____
- supply an outline of what allowance and savings will be used for

(Parent) I, _____ will:
- pay $ _____ allowance every Sunday/Monday
- receive an outline of what allowance will be used for
- receive an outline of what savings will be used for: short and long term

I, _____ will use my allowance for the following:
-
-
-
-
-

I, _____ will use my savings for the following:
-
-
-
-
-

_____   _____
Child   Parent

_____   _____
Date   Date

Allowance Tracker

Date	Child #1	Child #2	Child #3
January			
Week #1			
Week #2			
Week #3			
Week #4			
Week #5			
Other Job(s)			
February			
Week #1			
Week #2			
Week #3			
Week #4			
Week #5			
Other Job(s)			
March			
Week #1			
Week #2			
Week #3			
Week #4			
Week #5			
Other Job(s)			
April			
Week #1			
Week #2			
Week #3			
Week #4			
Week #5			
Other Job(s)			

Allowance Tracker (cont'd)

Date	Child #1	Child #2	Child #3
May			
Week #1			
Week #2			
Week #3			
Week #4			
Week #5			
Other Job(s)			
June			
Week #1			
Week #2			
Week #3			
Week #4			
Week #5			
Other Job(s)			
July			
Week #1			
Week #2			
Week #3			
Week #4			
Week #5			
Other Job(s)			
August			
Week #1			
Week #2			
Week #3			
Week #4			
Week #5			
Other Job(s)			

Allowance Tracker (cont'd)

Date	Child #1	Child #2	Child #3
September			
Week #1			
Week #2			
Week #3			
Week #4			
Week #5			
Other Job(s)			
October			
Week #1			
Week #2			
Week #3			
Week #4			
Week #5			
Other Job(s)			
November			
Week #1			
Week #2			
Week #3			
Week #4			
Week #5			
Other Job(s)			
December			
Week #1			
Week #2			
Week #3			
Week #4			
Week #5			
Other Job(s)			

The Wise Purchase Plotter

Item	Choices	Cost	Pros	Cons
	1			
	2			
	3			
	1			
	2			
	3			
	1			
	2			
	3			
	1			
	2			
	3			
	1			
	2			
	3			
	1			
	2			
	3			
	1			
	2			
	3			

The Kid's Vacation Planner

Destination	
Departure Date	
Dollar Goal	
Weekly Contribution	

Date	Deposit	Total

The Kid's Inventory

Name:_____

✔	I Want	✔	I Need	✔	I Have

The Gift of Giving

THREE WAYS I CAN HELP OTHERS:

Money

I will donate $_____ a week/month to the following local charity or organization:

_____

Time

I will volunteer my time to the following community group or organization:

_____

Date:_____

Time per week/month/year:_____

Clothes and Toys

I will donate unused clothes & toys to the following local charity or organization:

_____

The Kid's Loan Contract

(Parent) I, _____ will loan (child) _____ (amount) $ _____ to

purchase _____ .

THE TERMS OF THE REPAYMENT ARE AS FOLLOWS:

(Child) I, _____ will pay (amount) $ _____ per (week, month) _____

for (#) _____ (weeks, months) _____ , commencing (date) _____ .

_____
Child

_____
Parent

_____
Date

_____
Date

Note:
1. Chores _____
2. Work _____
3. _____

The Kid's Loan Repayment Planner

AGREEMENT BETWEEN:

_____ (child) & _____ (parent)

TOTAL AMOUNT OF LOAN:

$_____

Date	Amount	Cumulative

REPAYMENT TO BE MADE IN FULL ON OR BEFORE

_____

The Kid's Cash Flow

	Annual	Monthly
Income		
Allowance		
Gift Money		
Work Money		
Expenses		
Entertainment		
Lunches/Snacks		
Movies/Arcades		
Hobbies/School		
Magazines		
Music		
School Activities		
Gifts		
Birthdays		
Christmas/Other Occasions		
Transportation		
Bus fare		
Vacation		
Savings		
Miscellaneous		

The Kid's Investment Calculator

Date	Amount	Source (Allowance, Job, Gift)	Cumulative Savings Total

The Kid's Business Builder

Name of Business:
Mission Statement:
Your Product or Service:
Price:
Reasons Why it is Worth the Price:
1.
2.
3.

The Business Mind Map

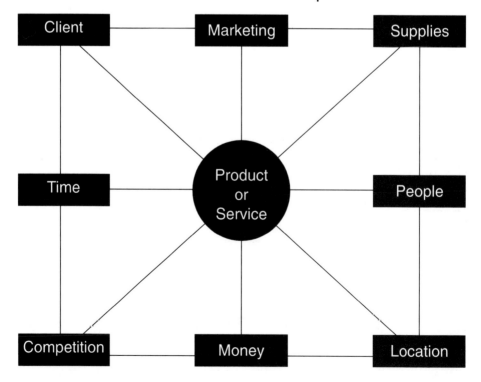

The Critical Decision Maker

Top 20 Wishes

Wish	Rating (1-10)	Pros	Cons	Order of Priority

Top 5 Wishes

Wish	Target Date	Actions to Achieve

The Teen Purchase Plan

Item	Need/Want	Total Cost	Parents' Contribution	Child's Contribution

Teen Cash Flow

	Annual	Monthly
Income		
Employment/Business		
Allowance		
Gift Money		
Awards/Prizes		
Expenses		
Entertainment		
Lunches		
Movies/Arcades		
Eating Out		
Events/Concerts		
Hobbies/School		
Magazines		
Music		
School Activities		
Clothing		
School		
Party		
Work		
Sports		
Fees		
Equipment/Uniforms		
Personal Care		
Hair Cuts		
Make-Up		
Gifts		
Birthdays		
Christmas		
Communication		
Home Phone/Long Distance		
Cell/Pager		
Transportation		
Gas/Oil/Insurance		
Bus Fare		
Savings		
Miscellaneous		

OTHER RESOURCES

Related Readings

Axelrod, Amy, and Sharon McGinley-Nally. *Pigs Will Be Pigs* (Prentice-Hall, 1998).

Chilton, David. *The Wealthy Barber.* (Toronto: Stoddart Publishing Co. Ltd., 1989)

Drew, Bonnie. *Show Me the Money: 101 Money-Making Projects for Kids* (Summit Financial Products Inc., 1998).

Drew, Bonnie and Noel. *Fast Cash for Kids* (Career Press Inc., 1995).

Godfrey, Neale S. *The Kids Money Book* (Checkerboard Press Inc., 1991).

McLean, Benjamin. *Guarantee Your Child's Financial Future* (Whitby: McGraw-Hill Ryerson, 1998)

Peterson, Jean Ross. *It Doesn't Grow on Trees* (FNW Publications, 1988).

Roper, Ingrid. *Moneymakers: Good Sense for Girls* (Pleasant Company Publications, 1998).

Trapani, Iza. *How Much is that Doggie in the Window?* (Whispering Coyote Press, 1997).

Vaz-Oxlade, Gail. *The Money Tree Myth* (General Distribution Services, 1996).

Weinstein, Grace W. *Lifetime Book of Money Management* (Visible Press, 1993).

Chicken Soup for the Teenage Soul (Health Communications, 1997.

Willy Wonka and the Chocolate Factory.

Related Web Sites

The following Web sites are a good source of information on teaching children about money; many also offer helpful links to other sites on the Internet.

www.agf.com/financial_lifeskills

www.halifax.cbc.ca/streetcents

www.hsx.com

www.kidsmoneystore.com

www.kolbe.com

www.pages.prodigy.com/kidsmoney

www.parentsoup.com

Related Games

The following games will help you and your family put some of the ideas and goals in this book into practice in a relaxing and fun environment.

Careers - ages 10+

Fame, fortune and happiness

Game of Life, The - ages 9+

Learn to dodge bad luck and make some money. Money is earned by doing good deeds, helping the community or taking a break.

Jenga

Build your money like a tower, by taking it from one place and putting it where it will be more useful.

Mall Madness - ages 9+

Teaches children how to use money and credit cards, how to resist impulse shopping and the importance of making lists.

Money Cents - ages 5+

Teaches basic money skills. Children answer basic money questions and learn the value of each coin, how to count and about gaining and losing money.

Monopoly - ages 8+

Teaches children the concepts of money and how to deal with it through buying and selling. Children also learn the value of money.

Payday - ages 8+

A family game that makes family finances fun. Teaches children where household money goes.

Risk - ages 10+

Teaches about calculated risks. Helpful in viewing the differences of risks versus playing it safe (e.g. stocks vs. savings).

Stock Ticker - ages 9+

Buying and selling of stocks.

Wall Street

Teaches the family about playing the stock market.

Related Resources and Contacts

The Duke of Edinburgh Award
National Office:
Suite 406, P.O. Box 124
207 Queen's Quay West
Toronto, ON
M5J 1A7

phone: (416) 203-0674
              1(800) 872-3853
fax: (416) 203-0676
e-mail: duke@dukeofed.org
Web site: http://dukeofed.org/~duke

INDEX

ABOUT AUTHOR

Paul W. Lermitte, B.A., C.F.P., R.F.P.

Paul's interest in financial planning began when he bought his first Canada Savings Bond as an eight year old paper carrier. He continued to follow his passions by earning a Bachelor of Arts degree in Business in 1982. Since 1984, Paul has been advising individuals, business owners and family businesses in the creation and protection of wealth.

Paul is a partner of IFC Planning Group Inc. He is also a Registered Financial Planner, as well as a Certified Financial Planner. Paul is a shareholder of Assante Capital Management Inc. and a representative with FPC Investments Inc., a registered securities dealer. He is licensed in both Life and Disability Insurance as well as Securities. Paul is also a practitioner member of the Canadian Association of Financial Planners and a member of the International Association of Financial Planners.

Paul has been a participant in the Strategic Coach program for nine years and actively assists others with their growth at workshops. Paul has a passion for coaching on many levels: in financial matters, in business, in community sports and in church. Paul was a speaker at the IAFP "Success Forum" in 1997, on the topic, "Building Your Winning Team." He has also been a soccer coach for nine years and holds a Level Three Coaching Certification. He is Treasurer and past president for the South Arm Soccer Association and acts as coordinator for his church youth group. He also enjoys helping with the school track team.

Paul lives in Richmond, British Columbia, with his wife, Jan, and their three sons.

GREAT BOOKS FOR CANADIAN FAMILIES

How and WHEN to introduce children to the internet
Taking Your Kids ONLINE
DR. ARLETTE LEFEBVRE BRIAN HILLIS

0-07-560932-0
$22.99

THE CANADIAN CONSUMER'S GUIDE TO HEALTH CARE
HOW TO GET THE HEALTH CARE YOU NEED WHEN YOU NEED IT
become a savvy health care consumer ✤ get the best health care for you and your family ✤ pros and cons of alternative medicine ✤ when and how to seek a specialist ✤ pros and cons of complete hospital care
SHARON LINDENBURGER

0-07-560312-8
$19.99

Douglas Gray
Canadian
HOME BUYING MADE EASY
1 Buying your first home
2 Negotiating the best deal
3 Inspecting, closing, and moving in!

0-07-552900-9
$17.99

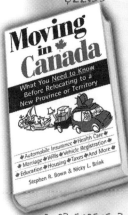

Moving in Canada
What You Need to Know Before Relocating to a New Province or Territory
✤ Automobile Insurance ✤ Health Care ✤
✤ Marriage ✤ Wills ✤ Vehicle Registration ✤
✤ Education ✤ Housing ✤ Taxes ✤ And More ✤
Stephen R. Bown & Nicky L. Brink

0-07-560545-7
$19.99

HOW TO RESEARCH
ALMOST ANYTHING
A Canadian Guide for Students, Consumers and Business
STEPHEN OVERBURY & SUSANNA BUENAVENTURA

0-07-560168-0
$19.99

GUARANTEE
YOUR CHILD'S FINANCIAL FUTURE
Practical Solutions for Today's Parents
✤ SAVE MONEY FOR COLLEGE OR UNIVERSITY
✤ BUILD A STRONG FINANCIAL SAFETY NET
✤ MAKE A WILL AND PROTECT YOUR ESTATE
✤ TEACH YOUR CHILDREN TO SAVE AND INVEST
BENJAMIN McLEAN

0-07-560410-8
$21.99

available at your local bookstore